MW00931926

Disclaimer:

The information contained within this book is strictly
for educational purposes. If you wish to apply ideas
contained in this book, you are taking full responsibility
for your actions. This book is not intended as a
substitute for the medical advice of physicians. The
author & publisher advise readers to take full
responsibility for their safety and know their limits.

# THE LESSER KEY OF SOLOMON

# LEMEGETON

## BOOKS I, II, III, IV, V

XVII CENTURY

AUTHOR UNKNOWN

I ENGLISH EDITION BY

S. L. MACGREGOR MATHERS, 1904

2021 EDITION EDITED, POLISHED &
ANNOTATED BY

R.W.Z.Y. ESOTERIC PRESS

# INTRODUCTION

*"The half-wise, recognizing the comparative unreality of the Universe, imagine that they may defy its Laws, such are vain and presumptuous fools, and they are broken against the rocks and torn asunder by the elements by reason of their folly. The truly wise, knowing the nature of the Universe, use Law against laws; the higher against the lower; and by the Art of Alchemy transmute that which is undesirable into that which is worthy, and thus triumph. Mastery consists not in abnormal dreams, visions and fantastic imaginings or living, but in using the higher forces against the lower, escaping the pains of the lower planes by vibrating on the higher. Transmutation, not presumptuous denial, is the weapon of the Master."* — The Kybalion, 1908.

Magick, with a "k" to distinguish it from the magic in fiction and the tricks performed by illusionists, is the study and understanding of the non-material Universe and its Laws and putting said knowledge to practical use.

There's not just one right way to achieve and use that knowledge, though. Specific practices identified as Magick are found worldwide through hystory. Spells, divination, rituals, communication with Spirits, &c. What's interesting to see is how the core of each of these methods is similar in every tradition and every part of the world both in the past and nowadays.

Many of those practices reached us thanks to books and manuscripts, called Grimoires (from the French *"grammaire"*). Some of these manuscripts date back as far as between the 5th and 4th centuries BC in Mesopotamia in the form of cuneiform clay tablets.

Some of the most known grimoires are the Solomonic Grimoires: The Lesser Key of Solomon & The Greater Key of Solomon.

The Lemegeton, also known as The Lesser Key of Solomon, is a collection of five grimoires dating back to at least 1500 and attributed to King Solomon: Ars Goetia, Ars Theurgia Goetia, Ars Paulina, Ars Almadel, and Ars Notoria.

Despite being attributed to Solomon, these grimoires' content comes from texts such as Pseudomonarchia Daemonum - appendix to De Praestigiis Daemonum - by J. Weyer, the Heptameron - or Magical Elements - by P.d'Abano, Steganographia by J. Trithemius, and other grimoires.

The Ars Goetia is the first grimoire of the Lemegeton. Its also known as Liber Malorum Spirituum. It contains the Names, Orders, Offices, Seals, and Characteristics of 72 Spirits - or Demons - and explains how to conjure them and how to protect yourself when doing so.
The Spirits of this grimoire are described as evil and the Ars Goetia - from the Greek term γοητεια (goēteia), meaning spell - itself is the art of conjuring this kind of spirits, opposed to the Theurgia - from the Greek term θεουργία (theurghía) - which is the evocation of Divine Spirits and Gods.

The Ars Theurgia Goetia is the second grimoire of the Lemegeton. It contains the Names, Seals, and Characteristics of 32 Aerial Spirits, both good and evil. Each one of these Spirits govern over a specific point of the compass.
The name of this grimoire is interesting as the term Theurgia is being improperly used. The term Theurgia is used here in combination with

the term Goetia to indicate the mixed nature of the Spirits of this grimoire, while the Theurgia was a practice exclusively used for the Gods and Divine Spirits.

The Ars Paulina is the third grimoire of the Lemegeton. It consists of two parts. The first part contains a system to invoke the Angels ruling over each planetary hour of the day and night. Each one of these 24 angels governs over several other Spirits, Dukes, who themselves rule over more Spirits. Only a selection of them is mentioned in this grimoire.

The second part explains how to invoke the Angel ruling over your birth, and it gives a list of each one of the 360 Angels ruling over each degree of the 12 zodiac signs.

The Ars Almadel is the fourth grimoire of the Lemegeton. It contains the system to conjure the Angels of the four Choras - or Altitudes - who rule over cardinal directions, equinoxes, solstices, and zodiac signs.

The Ars Nova, also called Ars Notoria, is the fifth and the last grimoire of the Lemegeton. It takes its name from the figures - notae - contained in the manuscript. It contains a system to acquire knowledge and skills such as grammar, languages, philosophy, science, geometry, and more. It's very different compared to the other grimoires of the Lemegeton and not all the manuscripts contain it.

This book will contain all of these five grimoires. I've decided to don't modernize the language of the source material and not to include critical commentary so the reader can make up their own idea about these grimoires.

# THE LESSER KEY OF SOLOMON

# LEMEGETON

## BOOK I, ARS GOETIA

SOURCE MATERIAL
"THE KEY OF SOLOMON THE KING", 1904

BY

S. L. MACGREGOR MATHERS

&

ALEISTER CROWLEY

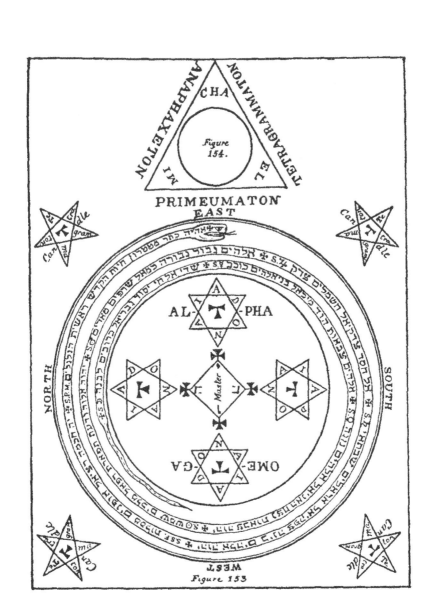
Figure 153

# INTRODUCTORY DESCRIPTION

THE WHOLE LEMEGETON OR CLAVICULA.

Now this Book containeth all the Names, Orders, and Offices of all the Spirits with which Solomon ever conversed, the Seals and Characters belonging to each Spirit, and the manner of calling them forth to visible appearance:

Divided into 5 special Books or parts, viz.:

1. THE FIRST BOOK, or PART, which is a Book concerning Spirits of Evil, and which is termed THE GOETIA OF SOLOMON, sheweth forth his manner of binding these Spirits for use in things divers. And hereby did he acquire great renown.

2. THE SECOND BOOK is one which treateth of Spirits mingled of Good and Evil Natures, the which is entitled THE THEURGIA-GOETIA, or the Magical Wisdom of the Spirits Aërial, whereof some do abide, but certain do wander and abide not.

3. THE THIRD BOOK, called ARS PAULINA, or THE ART PAULINE, treateth of the Spirits allotted unto every degree of the 360 Degrees of the Zodiac; and also of the Signs, and of the Planets in the Signs, as well as of the Hours.

4. THE FOURTH BOOK, called ARS ALMADEL SALOMONIS, or THE ART ALMADEL OF SOLOMON, concerneth those Spirits which be set over the Quaternary of the Altitudes.

These two last mentioned Books, the ART PAULINE and the ART ALMADEL, do relate unto Good Spirits alone, whose knowledge is to be obtained through seeking unto the Divine. These two Books be also classed together under the Name of the First and Second Parts of the Book THEURGIA OF SOLOMON.

5.THE FIFTH BOOK of the Lemegeton is one of Prayers and Orations. The which Solomon the Wise did use upon the Altar in the Temple. And the titles hereof be ARS NOVA, the NEW ART, and ARS NOTARIA, the NOTARY ART. The which was revealed to him by MICHAEL, that Holy Angel of God, in thunder and in lightning, and he further did receive by the aforesaid Angel certain Notes written by the Hand of God, without the which that Great King had never attained unto his great Wisdom, for thus he knew all things and all Sciences and Arts whether Good or Evil.

# THE 72 SPIRITS OF THE

# ARS GOETIA

# 1 - BAEL

The First Principal Spirit is a King ruling in the East, called Bael. He maketh thee to go Invisible. He ruleth over 66 Legions of Infernal Spirits. He appeareth in divers shapes, sometimes like a Cat, sometimes like a Toad, and sometimes like a Man, and sometimes all these forms at once. He speaketh hoarsely. This is his character which is used to be worn as a Lamen before him who calleth him forth, or else he will not do thee homage

# 2 - AGARES

The Second Spirit is a Duke called Agreas, or Agares. He is under the Power of the East, and cometh up in the form of an old fair Man, riding upon a Crocodile, carrying a Goshawk upon his fist, and yet mild in appearance. He maketh them to run that stand still, and bringeth back runaways. He teaches all Languages or Tongues presently. He hath power also to destroy Dignities both Spiritual and Temporal, and causeth Earthquakes. He was of the Order of Virtues. He hath under his government 31 Legions of Spirits. And this is his Seal or Character which thou shalt wear as a Lamen before thee.

# 3 - VASSAGO

The Third Spirit is a Mighty Prince, being of the same nature as Agares. He is called Vassago. This Spirit is of a Good Nature, and his office is to declare things Past and to Come, and to discover all things Hid or Lost. And he governeth 26 Legions of Spirits, and this is his Seal.

# 4 - SAMIGINA

The Fourth Spirit is Samigina, a Great Marquis. He appeareth in the form of a little Horse or Ass, and then into Human shape doth he change himself at the request of the Master. He speaketh with a hoarse voice. He ruleth over 30 Legions of Inferiors. He teaches all Liberal Sciences, and giveth account of Dead Souls that died in sin. And his Seal is this, which is to be worn before the Magician when he is Invocator, etc.

# 5 - MARBAS

The fifth Spirit is Marbas. He is a Great President, and appeareth at first in the form of a Great Lion, but afterwards, at the request of the Master, he putteth on Human Shape. He answereth truly of things Hidden or Secret. He causeth Diseases and cureth them. Again, he giveth great Wisdom and Knowledge in Mechanical Arts; and can change men into other shapes. He governeth 36 Legions of Spirits. And his Seal is this, which is to be worn as aforesaid.

# 6 - VALEFOR

The Sixth Spirit is Valefor. He is a mighty Duke, and appeareth in the shape of a Lion with an Ass's Head, bellowing. He is a good Familiar, but tempteth them he is a familiar of to steal. He governeth 10 Legions of Spirits. His Seal is this, which is to be worn, whether thou wilt have him for a Familiar, or not.

# 7 - AMON

The Seventh Spirit is Amon. He is a Marquis great in power, and most stern. He appeareth like a Wolf with a Serpent's tail, vomiting out of his mouth flames of fire; but at the command of the Magician he putteth on the shape of a Man with Dog's teeth beset in a head like a Raven; or else like a Man with a Raven's head (simply). He telleth all things Past and to Come. He procureth feuds and reconcileth controversies between friends. He governeth 40 Legions of Spirits. His Seal is this which is to be worn as aforesaid, etc.

# 8 - BARBATOS

The Eighth Spirit is Barbatos. He is a Great Duke, and appeareth when the Sun is in Sagittary, with four noble Kings and their companies of great troops. He giveth understanding of the singing of Birds, and of the Voices of other creatures, such as the barking of Dogs. He breaketh the Hidden Treasures open that have been laid by the Enchantments of Magicians. He is of the Order of Virtues, of which some part he retaineth still; and he knoweth all things Past, and to come, and conciliateth Friends and those that be in Power. He ruleth over 30 Legions of Spirits. His Seal of Obedience is this, the which wear before thee as aforesaid.

# 9 - PAIMON

The Ninth Spirit in this Order is Paimon, a Great King, and very obedient unto LUCIFER. He appeareth in the form of a Man sitting upon a Dromedary with a Crown most glorious upon his head. There goeth before him also an Host of Spirits, like Men with Trumpets and well sounding Cymbals, and all other sorts of Musical Instruments. He hath a great Voice, and roareth at his first coming, and his speech is such that the Magician cannot well understand unless he can compel him. This Spirit can teach all Arts and Sciences, and other secret things. He can discover unto thee what the Earth is, and what holdeth it up in the Waters; and what Mind is, and where it is; or any other thing thou mayest desire to know.

He giveth Dignity, and confirmeth the same. He bindeth or maketh any man subject unto the Magician if he so desire it. He giveth good Familiars, and such as can teach all Arts. He is to be observed towards the West. He is of the Order of Dominations. He hath under him 200 Legions of Spirits, and part of them are of the Order of Angels, and the other part of Potentates. Now if thou callest this Spirit Paimon alone, thou must make him some offering; and there will attend him two Kings called LABAL and ABALI , and also other Spirits who be of the Order of Potentates in his Host, and 25 Legions. And those Spirits which be subject unto them are not always with them unless the Magician do compel them. His Character is this which must be worn as a Lamen before thee, etc.

# 10 - BUER

The Tenth Spirit is Buer, a Great President. He appeareth in Sagittary, and that is his shape when the Sun is there. He teaches Philosophy, both Moral and Natural, and the Logic Art, and also the Virtues of all Herbs and Plants. He healeth all distempers in man, and giveth good Familiars. He governeth 50 Legions of Spirits, and his Character of obedience is this, which thou must wear when thou callest him forth unto appearance.

# 11 - GUSION

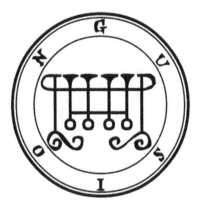

The Eleventh Spirit in order is a great and strong Duke, called Gusion. He appeareth like a Xenopilus. He telleth all things, Past, Present, and to Come, and showeth the meaning and resolution of all questions thou mayest ask. He conciliateth and reconcileth friendships, and giveth Honour and Dignity unto any. He ruleth over 40 Legions of Spirits. His Seal is this, the which wear thou as aforesaid.

# 12 - SITRI

The Twelfth Spirit is Sitri. He is a Great Prince and appeareth at first with a Leopard's head and the Wings of a Gryphon, but after the command of the Master of the Exorcism he putteth on Human shape, and that very beautiful. He enflameth men with Women's love, and Women with Men's love; and causeth them also to show themselves naked if it be desired. He governeth 60 Legions of Spirits. His Seal is this, to be worn as a Lamen before thee, etc.

# 13 - BELETH

The Thirteenth Spirit is called Beleth (or Bileth, or Bilet). He is a mighty King and terrible. He rideth on a pale horse with trumpets and other kinds of musical instruments playing before him. He is very furious at his first appearance, that is, while the Exorcist layeth his courage; for to do this he must hold a Hazel Wand in his hand, striking it out towards the South and East Quarters, make a triangle, $\triangle$, without the Circle, and then command him into it by the Bonds and Charges of Spirits as hereafter followeth. And if he doth not enter into the triangle, $\triangle$, at your threats, rehearse the Bonds and Charms before him, and then he will yield Obedience and come into it, and do what he is commanded by the Exorcist. Yet he must receive him courteously because he is a Great King,

and do homage unto him, as the Kings and Princes do that attend upon him. And thou must have always a Silver Ring on the middle finger of the left hand held against thy face, as they do yet before AMAYMON. This Great King Beleth causeth all the love that may be, both of Men and of Women, until the Master Exorcist hath had his desire fulfilled. He is of the Order of Powers, and he governeth 85 Legions of Spirits. His Noble Seal is this, which is to be worn before thee at working.

# 14 - LERAJE

The Fourteenth Spirit is called Leraje (or Leraie). He is a Marquis Great in Power, showing himself in the likeness of an Archer clad in Green, and carrying a Bow and Quiver. He causeth all great Battles and Contests; and maketh wounds to putrefy that are made with Arrows by Archers. This belongeth unto Sagittary. He governeth 30 Legions of Spirits, and this is his Seal, etc.

# 15 - ELIGOS

The Fifteenth Spirit in Order is Eligos, a Great Duke, and appeareth in the form of a goodly Knight, carrying a Lance, an Ensign, and a Serpent. He discovereth hidden things, and knoweth things to come; and of Wars, and how the Soldiers will or shall meet. He causeth the Love of Lords and Great Persons. He governeth 60 Legions of Spirits. His Seal is this, etc.

# 16 - ZEPAR

The Sixteenth Spirit is Zepar. He is a Great Duke, and appeareth in Red Apparel and Armour, like a Soldier. His office is to cause Women to love Men, and to bring them together in love. He also maketh them barren. He governeth 26 Legions of Inferior Spirits, and his Seal is this, which he obeyeth when he seeth it.

# 17 - BOTIS

The Seventeenth Spirit is Botis, a Great President, and an Earl. He appeareth at the first show in the form of an ugly Viper, then at the command of the Magician he putteth on a Human shape with Great Teeth, and two Horns, carrying a bright and sharp Sword in his hand. He telleth all things Past, and to Come, and reconcileth Friends and Foes. He ruleth over 60 Legions of Spirits, and this is his Seal, etc.

# 18 - BATHIN

The Eighteenth Spirit is Bathin. He is a Mighty and Strong Duke, and appeareth like a Strong Man with the tail of a Serpent, sitting upon a Pale-Coloured Horse. He knoweth the Virtues of Herbs and Precious Stones, and can transport men suddenly from one country to another. He ruleth over 30 Legions of Spirits. His Seal is this which is to be worn as aforesaid.

# 19 - SALLOS

The Nineteenth Spirit is Sallos (or Saleos). He is a Great and Mighty Duke, and appeareth in the form of a gallant Soldier riding on a Crocodile, with a Ducal Crown on his head, but peaceably. He causeth the Love of Women to Men, and of Men to Women; and governeth 30 Legions of Spirits. His Seal is this, etc.

# 20 - PURSON

The Twentieth Spirit is Purson, a Great King. His appearance is comely, like a Man with a Lion's face, carrying a cruel Viper in his hand, and riding upon a Bear. Going before him are many Trumpets sounding. He knoweth all things hidden, and can discover Treasure, and tell all things Past, Present, and to Come. He can take a Body either Human or Aërial, and answereth truly of all Earthly things both Secret and Divine, and of the Creation of the World. He bringeth forth good Familiars, and under his Government there be 22 Legions of Spirits, partly of the Order of Virtues and partly of the Order of Thrones. His Mark, Seal, or Character is this, unto the which he oweth obedience, and which thou shalt wear in time of action, etc.

# 21 - MARAX

The Twenty-first Spirit is Marax. He is a Great Earl and President. He appeareth like a great Bull with a Man's face. His office is to make Men very knowing in Astronomy, and all other Liberal Sciences; also he can give good Familiars, and wise, knowing the virtues of Herbs and Stones which be precious. He governeth 30 Legions of Spirits, and his Seal is this, which must be made and worn as aforesaid, etc.

# 22 - IPOS

The Twenty-second Spirit is lpos. He is an Earl, and a Mighty Prince, and appeareth in the form of an Angel with a Lion's Head, and a Goose's Foot, and Hare's Tail. He knoweth all things Past, Present, and to Come. He maketh men witty and bold. He governeth 36 Legions of Spirits. His Seal is this, which thou shalt wear, etc.

# 23 - AIM

The Twenty-third Spirit is Aim. He is a Great Strong Duke. He appeareth in the form of a very handsome Man in body, but with three Heads; the first, like a Serpent, the second like a Man having two Stars on his Forehead, the third like a Calf. He rideth on a Viper, carrying a Firebrand in his Hand, wherewith he setteth cities, castles, and great Places, on fire. He maketh thee witty in all manner of ways, and giveth true answers unto private matters. He governeth 26 Legions of Inferior Spirits; and his Seal is this, which wear thou as aforesaid, etc.

# 24 - NABERIUS

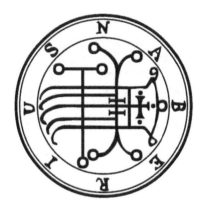

The Twenty-fourth Spirit is Naberius. He is a most valiant Marquis, and showeth in the form of a Black Crane, fluttering about the Circle, and when he speaketh it is with a hoarse voice. He maketh men cunning in all Arts and Sciences, but especially in the Art of Rhetoric. He restoreth lost Dignities and Honours. He governeth 19 Legions of Spirits. His Seal is this, which is to be worn, etc.

# 25 - GLASYA-LABOLAS

The Twenty-fifth Spirit is Glasya-Labolas. He is a Mighty President and Earl, and showeth himself in the form of a Dog with Wings like a Gryphon. He teacheth all Arts and Sciences in an instant, and is an Author of Bloodshed and Manslaughter. He teacheth all things Past, and to Come. If desired he causeth the love both of Friends and of Foes. He can make a Man to go Invisible. And he hath under his command 36 Legions of Spirits. His Seal is this, to be, etc.

# 26 - BUNE

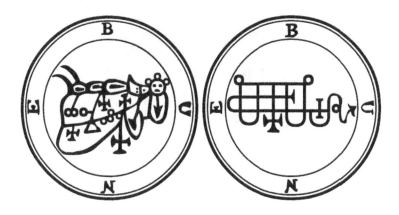

The Twenty-sixth Spirit is Bune (or Bim). He is a Strong, Great and Mighty Duke. He appeareth in the form of a Dragon with three heads, one like a Dog, one like a Gryphon, and one like a Man. He speaketh with a high and comely Voice. He changeth the Place of the Dead, and causeth the Spirits which be under him to gather together upon your Sepulchres. He giveth Riches unto a Man, and maketh him Wise and Eloquent. He giveth true Answers unto Demands. And he governeth 30 Legions of Spirits. His Seal is this, unto the which he oweth Obedience. He hath another Seal (which is the first of these, but the last is the best).

# 27 - RONOVE

The Twenty-seventh Spirit is Ronove. He appeareth in the Form of a Monster. He teacheth the Art of Rhetoric very well and giveth Good Servants, Knowledge of Tongues, and Favours with Friends or Foes. He is a Marquis and Great Earl; and there be under his command 19 Legions of Spirits. His Seal is this, etc.

# 28 - BERITH

The Twenty-eighth Spirit in Order, as Solomon bound them, is named
Berith. He is a Mighty, Great, and Terrible Duke. He hath two other
Names given unto him by men of later times, viz.: BEALE, or BEAL, and
BOFRY or BOLFRY. He appeareth in the Form of a Soldier with Red
Clothing, riding upon a Red Horse, and having a Crown of Gold upon
his head. He giveth true answers, Past, Present, and to Come. Thou
must make use of a Ring in calling him forth, as is before spoken of
regarding Beleth. He can turn all metals into Gold. He can give
Dignities, and can confirm them unto Man. He speaketh with a, very
clear and subtle Voice. He governeth 26 Legions of Spirits. His Seal is
this, etc.

# 29 - ASTAROTH

The Twenty-ninth Spirit is Astaroth. He is a Mighty, Strong Duke, and appeareth in the Form of an hurtful Angel riding on an Infernal Beast like a Dragon, and carrying in his right hand a Viper. Thou must in no wise let him approach too near unto thee, lest he do thee damage by his Noisome Breath. Wherefore the Magician must hold the Magical Ring near his face, and that will defend him. He giveth true answers of things Past, Present, and to Come, and can discover all Secrets. He will declare wittingly how the Spirits fell, if desired, and the reason of his own fall. He can make men wonderfully knowing in all Liberal Sciences. He ruleth 40 Legions of Spirits. His Seal is this, which wear thou as a Lamen before thee, or else he will not appear nor yet obey thee, etc.

# 30 - FORNEUS

The Thirtieth Spirit is Forneus. He is a Mighty and Great Marquis, and appeareth in the Form of a Great Sea-Monster. He teacheth, and maketh men wonderfully knowing in the Art of Rhetoric. He causeth men to have a Good Name, and to have the knowledge and understanding of Tongues. He maketh one to be beloved of his Foes as well as of his Friends. He governeth 29 Legions of Spirits, partly of the Order of Thrones, and partly of that of Angels. His Seal is this, which wear thou, etc.

# 31 - FORAS

The Thirty-first Spirit is Foras. He is a Mighty President, and appeareth in the Form of a Strong Man in Human Shape. He can give the understanding to Men how they may know the Virtues of all Herbs and Precious Stones. He teacheth the Arts of Logic and Ethics in all their parts. If desired he maketh men invisible, and to live long, and to be eloquent. He can discover Treasures and recover things Lost. He ruleth over 29 Legions of Spirits, and his Seal is this, which wear thou, etc.

# 32 - ASMODAY

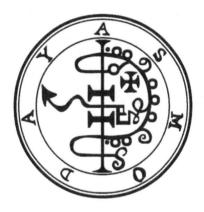

The Thirty-second Spirit is Asmoday, or Asmodai. He is a Great King, Strong, and Powerful. He appeareth with Three Heads, whereof the first is like a Bull, the second like a Man, and the third like a Ram; he hath also the tail of a Serpent, and from his mouth issue Flames of Fire. His Feet are webbed like those of a Goose. He sitteth upon an Infernal Dragon, and beareth in his hand a Lance with a Banner. He is first and choicest under the Power of AMAYMON, he goeth before all other. When the Exorcist hath a mind to call him, let it be abroad, and let him stand on his feet all the time of action, with his Cap or Headdress off; for if it be on, AMAYMON will deceive him and call all his actions to be bewrayed. But as soon as the Exorcist seeth Asmoday in the shape aforesaid, he shall call him by his Name, saying: "Art thou Asmoday?"

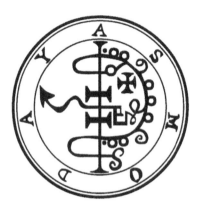

and he will not deny it, and by-and-by he will bow down unto the ground. He giveth the Ring of Virtues; he teacheth the Arts of Arithmetic, Astronomy, Geometry, and all handicrafts absolutely. He giveth true and full answers unto thy demands. He maketh one Invincible. He showeth the place where Treasures lie, and guardeth it. He, amongst the Legions of AMAYMON governeth 72 Legions of Spirits Inferior. His Seal is this which thou must wear as a Lamen upon thy breast, etc.

# 33 - GAAP

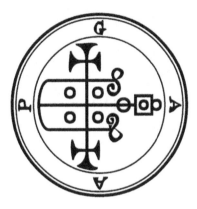

The Thirty-third Spirit is Gaap. He is a Great President and a Mighty Prince. He appeareth when the Sun is in some of the Southern Signs, in a Human Shape, going before Four Great and Mighty Kings, as if lie were a Guide to conduct them along on their way. His Office is to make men Insensible or Ignorant; as also in Philosophy to make them Knowing, and in all the Liberal Sciences. He can cause Love or Hatred, also he can teach thee to consecrate those things that belong to the Dominion of AMAYMON his King. He can deliver Familiars out of the Custody of other Magicians, and answereth truly and perfectly of things Past, Present, and to Come. He can carry and re-carry men very speedily from one Kingdom to another, at the Will and Pleasure of the Exorcist. He ruleth over 66 Legions of Spirits, and he was of the Order of Potentates. His Seal is this to be made and to be worn as aforesaid, etc.

# 34 - FURFUR

The Thirty-fourth Spirit is Furfur. He is a Great and Mighty Earl, appearing in the Form of an Hart with a Fiery Tail. He never speaketh truth unless he be compelled, or brought up within a triangle, $\triangle$ . Being therein, he will take upon himself the Form of an Angel. Being bidden, he speaketh with a hoarse voice. Also he will wittingly urge Love between Man and Woman. He can raise Lightnings and Thunders, Blasts, and Great Tempestuous Storms. And he giveth True Answers both of Things Secret and Divine, if commanded. He ruleth over 26 Legions of Spirits. And his Seal is this, etc.

# 35 - MARCHOSIAS

The Thirty-fifth Spirit is Marchosias. He is a Great and Mighty Marquis, appearing at first in the Form of a Wolf having Gryphon's Wings, and a Serpent's Tail, and Vomiting Fire out of his mouth. But after a time, at the command of the Exorcist he putteth on the Shape of a Man. And he is a strong fighter. He was of the Order of Dominations. He governeth 30 Legions of Spirits. He told his Chief, who was Solomon, that after 1,200 years he had hopes to return unto the Seventh Throne. And his Seal is this, to be made and worn as a Lamen, etc.

# 36 - STOLAS

The Thirty-sixth Spirit is Stolas, or Stolos. He is a Great and Powerful Prince, appearing in the Shape of a Mighty Raven at first before the Exorcist; but after he taketh the image of a Man. He teacheth the Art of Astronomy, and the Virtues of Herbs and Precious Stones. He governeth 26 Legions of Spirits; and his Seal is this, which is, etc.

# 37 - PHENEX

The Thirty-Seventh Spirit is Phenex (or Pheynix). He is a great Marquis, and appeareth like the Bird Phoenix, having the Voice of a Child. He singeth many sweet notes before the Exorcist, which he must not regard, but by-and-by he must bid him put on Human Shape. Then he will speak marvellously of all wonderful Sciences if required. He is a Poet, good and excellent. And he will be willing to perform thy requests. He hath hopes also to return to the Seventh Throne after 1,200 years more, as he said unto Solomon. He governeth 20 Legions of Spirits. And his Seal is this, which wear thou, etc.

# 38 - HALPHAS

The Thirty-eighth Spirit is Halphas, or Malthous (or Malthas). He is a Great Earl, and appeareth in the Form of a Stock-Dove. He speaketh with a hoarse Voice. His Office is to build up Towers, and to furnish them with Ammunition and Weapons, and to send Men-of-War to places appointed. He ruleth over 26 Legions of Spirits, and his Seal is this, etc.

# 39 - MALPHAS

The Thirty-ninth Spirit is Malphas. He appeareth at first like a Crow, but after he will put on Human Shape at the request of the Exorcist, and speak with a hoarse Voice. He is a Mighty President and Powerful. He can build Houses and High Towers, and can bring to thy Knowledge Enemies' Desires and Thoughts, and that which they have done. He giveth Good Familiars. If thou makest a Sacrifice unto him he will receive it kindly and willingly, but he will deceive him- that doth it. He governeth 40 Legions of Spirits, and his Seal is this, etc.

# 40 - RAUM

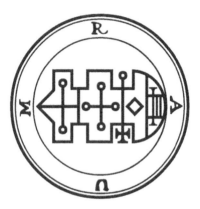

The Fortieth Spirit is Raum. He is a Great Earl; and appeareth at first in the Form of a Crow, but after the Command of the Exorcist he putteth on Human Shape. His office is to steal Treasures out King's Houses, and to carry it whither he is commanded, and to destroy Cities and Dignities of Men, and to tell all things, Past and What Is, and what Will Be; and to cause Love between Friends and Foes. He was of the Order of Thrones. He governeth 30 Legions of Spirits; and his Seal is this, which wear thou as aforesaid.

# 41 - FOCALOR

The Forty-first Spirit is Focalor, or Forcalor, or Furcalor. He is a Mighty Duke and Strong. He appeareth in the Form of a Man with Gryphon's Wings. His office is to slay Men, and to drown them in the Waters, and to overthrow Ships of War, for he hath Power over both Winds and Seas; but he will not hurt any man or thing if he be commanded to the contrary by the Exorcist. He also hath hopes to return to the Seventh Throne after 1,000 years. He governeth 30 Legions of Spirits, and his Seal is this, etc.

# 42 - VEPAR

The Forty-second Spirit is Vepar, or Vephar. He is a Duke Great and Strong and appeareth like a Mermaid. His office is to govern the Waters, and to guide Ships laden with Arms, Armour, and Ammunition, etc., thereon. And at the request of the Exorcist he can cause the seas to be right stormy and to appear full of ships. Also he maketh men to die in Three Days by Putrefying Wounds or Sores, and causing Worms to breed in them. He governeth 29 Legions of Spirits, and his Seal is this, etc.

# 43 - SABNOCK

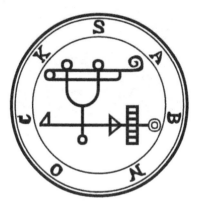

The Forty-third Spirit, as King Solomon commanded them into the Vessel of Brass, is called Sabnock, or Savnok. He is a Marquis, Mighty, Great and Strong, appearing in the Form of an Armed Soldier with a Lion's Head, riding on a pale-coloured horse. His office is to build high Towers, Castles and Cities, and-to furnish them with Armour, etc. Also he can afflict Men for many days with Wounds and with Sores rotten and full of Worms. He giveth Good Familiars at the request of the Exorcist. He commandeth 50 Legions of Spirits; and his Seal is this.

# 44 - SHAX

The Forty-fourth Spirit is Shax, or Shaz (or Shass). He is a Great Marquis and appeareth in the Form of a Stock-Dove, speaking with a voice hoarse, but yet subtle. His Office is to take away the Sight, Hearing, or Understanding of any Man or Woman at the command of the Exorcist; and to steal money out of the houses of Kings, and to carry it again in 1,200 years. If commanded he will fetch Horses at the request of the Exorcist, or any other thing. But he must first be commanded into a Triangle, $\triangle$, or else he will deceive him, and tell him many Lies. He can discover all things that are Hidden, and not kept by Wicked Spirits. He giveth good Familiars, sometimes. He governeth 30 Legions of Spirits, and his Seal is this, etc.

# 45 - VINE

The Forty-fifth Spirit is Vine, or Vinea. He is a Great King, and an Earl; and appeareth in the Form of a Lion, riding upon a Black Horse, and bearing a Viper in his hand. His Office is to discover Things Hidden, Witches, Wizards, and Things Present, Past, and to Come. He, at the command of the Exorcist will build Towers, overthrow Great Stone Walls, and make the Waters rough with Storms. He governeth 36 Legions of Spirits. And his Seal is this, which wear thou, as aforesaid, etc.

# 46 - BIFRONS

The Forty-sixth Spirit is called Bifrons, or Bifrous, or Bifrovs. He is an Earl, and appeareth in the Form of a Monster; but after a while, at the Command of the Exorcist, he putteth on the shape of a Man. His Office is to make one knowing in Astrology, Geometry, and other Arts and Sciences. He teacheth the Virtues of Precious Stones and Woods. He changeth Dead Bodies, and putteth them in another place; also he lighteth seeming Candles upon the Graves of the Dead. He hath under his Command 6 Legions of Spirits. His Seal is this, which he will own and submit unto, etc.

# 47 - VUAL

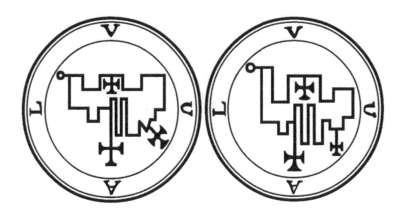

The Forty-seventh Spirit Uvall, or Vual, or Voval. He is a Duke, Great, Mighty, and Strong; and appeareth in the Form of a Mighty Dromedary at the first, but after a while at the Command of the Exorcist he putteth on Human Shape, and speaketh the Egyptian Tongue, but not perfectly. His Office is to procure the Love of Woman, and to tell Things Past, Present, and to Come. He also procureth Friendship between Friends and Foes. He was of the Order of Potestates or Powers. He governeth 37 Legions of Spirits, and his Seal is this, to be made and worn before thee, etc.

# 48 - HAAGENTI

The Forty-eighth Spirit is Haagenti. He is a President, appearing in the Form of a Mighty Bull with Gryphon's Wings. This is at first, but after, at the Command of the Exorcist he putteth on Human Shape. His Office is to make Men wise, and to instruct them in divers things; also to Transmute all Metals into Gold; and to change Wine into Water, and Water into Wine. He governeth 33 Legions of Spirits, and his Seal is this, etc.

# 49 - CROCELL

The Forty-ninth Spirit is Crocell, or Crokel. He appeareth in the Form of an Angel. He is a Duke Great and Strong, speaking something Mystically of Hidden Things. He teacheth the Art of Geometry and the Liberal Sciences. He, at the Command of the Exorcist, will produce Great Noises like the Rushings of many Waters, although there be none. He warmeth Waters, and discovereth Baths. He was of the Order of Potestates, or Powers, before his fall, as he declared unto the King Solomon. He governeth 48 Legions of Spirits. His Seal is this, the which wear thou as aforesaid.

# 50 - FURCAS

The Fiftieth Spirit is Furcas. He is a Knight, and appeareth in the Form of a Cruel Old Man with a long Beard and a hoary Head, riding upon a pale-coloured Horse, with a Sharp Weapon in his hand. His Office is to teach the Arts of Philosophy, Astrology, Rhetoric, Logic, Cheiromancy, and Pyromancy, in all their parts, and perfectly. He hath under his Power 20 Legions of Spirits. His Seal, or Mark, is thus made, etc.

# 51 - BALAM

The Fifty-first Spirit is Balam or Balaam. He is a Terrible, Great, and Powerful King. He appeareth with three Heads: the first is like that of a Bull; the second is like that of a Man; the third is like that of a Ram. He hath the Tail of a Serpent, and Flaming Eyes. He rideth upon a furious Bear, and carrieth a Boshawk upon his Fist. He speaketh with a hoarse Voice, giving True Answers of Things Past, Present, and to Come. He maketh men to go Invisible, and also to be Witty. He governeth 40 Legions of Spirits. His Seal is this, etc.

# 52 - ALLOCES

The Fifty-second Spirit is Alloces, or Alocas. He is a Duke, Great, Mighty, and Strong, appearing in the Form of a Soldier riding upon a Great Horse. His Face is like that of a Lion, very Red, and having Flaming Eyes. His Speech is hoarse and very big. His Office is to teach the Art of Astronomy, and all the Liberal Sciences. He bringeth unto thee Good Familiars; also he ruleth over 36 Legions of Spirits. His Seal is this, which, etc.

# 53 - CAMIO

The Fifty-third Spirit is Camio, or Caim. He is a Great President, and appeareth in the Form of the Bird called a Thrush at first, but afterwards he putteth on the Shape of a Man carrying in his Hand a Sharp Sword. He seemeth to answer in Burning Ashes, or in Coals of Fire. He is a Good Disputer. His Office is to give unto Men the Understanding of all Birds, Lowing of Bullocks, Barking of Dogs, and other Creatures; and also of the Voice of the Waters. He giveth True Answers of Things to Come. He was of the Order of Angels, but now ruleth over 30 Legions of Spirits Infernal. His Seal is this, which wear thou, etc

# 54 - MURMUR

The Fifty-fourth Spirit is called Murmur, or Murmus, or Murmux. He is a Great Duke, and an Earl; and appeareth in the Form of a Warrior riding upon a. Gryphon, with a Ducal Crown upon his Head. There do go before him those his Ministers, with great Trumpets sounding. His Office is to teach Philosophy perfectly, and to constrain Souls Deceased to come before the Exorcist to answer those questions which he may wish to put to them, if desired. He was partly of the Order of Thrones, and partly of that of Angels. He now ruleth 30 Legions of Spirits. And his Seal is this, etc.

# 55 - OROBAS

The Fifty-fifth Spirit is Orobas. He is a great and Mighty Prince, appearing at first like a Horse; but after the command of the Exorcist he putteth on the Image of a Man. His Office is to discover all things Past, Present, and to Come; also to give Dignities, and Prelacies, and the Favour of Friends and of Foes. He giveth True Answers of Divinity, and of the Creation of the World. He is very faithful unto the Exorcist, and will not suffer him to be tempted of any Spirit. He governeth 20 Legions of Spirits. His Seal is this, etc.

# 56 - GREMORY

The Fifty-sixth Spirit is Gremory, or Gamori. He is a Duke Strong and Powerful, and appeareth in the Form of a Beautiful Woman, with a Duchess's Crown tied about her waist, and riding on a Great Camel. His Office is to tell of all Things Past, Present, and to Come; and of Treasures Hid, and what they lie in; and to procure the Love of Women both Young and Old. He governeth 26 Legions of Spirits, and his Seal is this, etc.

# 57 - OSE

The Fifty-seventh Spirit is Oso, Ose, or Voso. He is a Great President, and appeareth like a Leopard at the first, but after a little time he putteth on the Shape of a Man. His Office is to make one cunning in the Liberal Sciences, and to give True Answers of Divine and Secret Things; also to change a Man into any Shape that the Exorcist pleaseth, so that he that is so changed will not think any other thing than that he is in verity that Creature or Thing he is changed into. He governeth 30 Legions of Spirits, and this is his Seal, etc.

# 58 - AMY

The Fifty-eighth Spirit is Amy, or Avnas. He is a Great President, and appeareth at first in the Form of a Flaming Fire; but after a while he putteth on the Shape of a Man. His office is to make one Wonderful Knowing in Astrology and all the Liberal Sciences. He giveth Good Familiars, and can bewray Treasure that is kept by Spirits. He governeth 36 Legions of Spirits, and his Seal is this, etc.

# 59 - ORIAS

The Fifty-ninth Spirit is Oriax, or Orias. He is a Great Marquis, and appeareth in the Form of a Lion, riding upon a Horse Mighty and Strong, with a Serpent's Tail; and he holdeth in his Right Hand two Great Serpents hissing. His Office is to teach the Virtues of the Stars, and to know the Mansions of the Planets, and how to understand their Virtues. He also transformeth Men, and he giveth Dignities, Prelacies, and Confirmation thereof; also Favour with Friends and with Foes. He doth govern 30 Legions of Spirits; and his Seal is this, etc.

# 60 - VAPULA

The Sixtieth Spirit is Vapula, or Naphula. He is a Duke Great, Mighty, and Strong; appearing in the Form of a Lion with Gryphon's Wings. His Office is to make Men Knowing in all Handcrafts and Professions, also in Philosophy, and other Sciences. He governeth 36 Legions of Spirits, and his Seal or Character is thus made, and thou shalt wear it as aforesaid, etc.

# 61 - ZAGAN

The Sixty-first Spirit is Zagan. He is a Great King and President, appearing at first in the Form of a Bull with Gryphon's Wings; but after a while he putteth on Human Shape. He maketh Men Witty. He can turn Wine into Water, and Blood into Wine, also Water into Wine. He can turn all Metals into Coin of the Dominion that Metal is of. He can even make Fools wise. He governeth 33 Legions of Spirits, and his Seal is this, etc.

# 62 - VALAC

The Sixty-second Spirit is Volac, or Valak, or Valu. He is a President Mighty and Great, and appeareth like a Child with Angel's Wings, riding on a Two-headed Dragon. His Office is to give True Answers of Hidden Treasures, and to tell where Serpents may be seen. The which he will bring unto the Exorciser without any Force or Strength being by him employed. He governeth 38 Legions of Spirits, and his Seal is thus.

# 63 - ANDRAS

The Sixty-third Spirit is Andras. He is a Great Marquis, appearing in the Form of an Angel with a Head like a Black Night Raven, riding upon a strong Black Wolf, and having a Sharp and Bright Sword flourished aloft in his hand. His Office is to sow Discords. If the Exorcist have not a care, he will slay both him and his fellows. He governeth 30 Legions of Spirits, and this is his Seal, etc.

# 64 - HAURES

The Sixty-fourth Spirit is Haures, or Hauras, or Havres, or Flauros. He is a Great Duke, and appeareth at first like a Leopard, Mighty, Terrible, and Strong, but after a while, at the Command of the Exorcist, he putteth on Human. Shape with Eyes Flaming and Fiery, and a most Terrible Countenance. He giveth True Answers of all things, Present, Past, and to Come. But if he be not commanded into a Triangle, $\triangle$, he will Lie in all these Things, and deceive and beguile the Exorcist in these things, or in such and such business. He will, lastly, talk of the Creation of the World, and of Divinity, and of how he and other Spirits fell. He destroyeth and burneth up those who be the Enemies of the Exorcist should he so desire it; also he will not suffer him to be tempted by any other Spirit or otherwise. He governeth 36 Legions of Spirits, and his Seal is this, to be worn as a Lamen, etc.

# 65 - ANDREALPHUS

The Sixty-fifth Spirit is Andrealphus. He is a Mighty Marquis, appearing at first in the form of a Peacock, with great Noises. But after a time he putteth on Human shape. He can teach Geometry perfectly. He maketh Men very subtle therein; and in all Things pertaining unto Mensuration or Astronomy. He can transform a Man into the Likeness of a Bird. He governeth 30 Legions of Infernal Spirits, and his Seal is this, etc

# 66 - CIMEIES

The Sixtysixth Spirit is Cimejes, or Cimeies, or Kimaris. He is a Marquis, Mighty, Great, Strong and Powerful, appearing like a Valiant Warrior riding upon a goodly Black Horse. He ruleth over all Spirits in the parts of Africa. His Office is to teach perfectly Grammar, Logic, Rhetoric, and to discover things Lost or Hidden, and Treasures. He governeth 20 Legions of Infernals; and his Seal is this, etc.

# 67 - AMDUSIAS

The Sixty-seventh Spirit is Amdusias, or Amdukias. He is a Duke Great and Strong, appearing at first like a Unicorn, but at the request of the Exorcist he standeth before him in Human Shape, causing Trumpets, and all manner of Musical Instruments to be heard, but not soon or immediately. Also he can cause Trees to bend and incline according to the Exorcist's Will. He giveth Excellent Familiars. He governeth 29 Legions of Spirits. And his Seal is this, etc.

# 68 - BELIAL

The Sixty-eighth Spirit is Belial. He is a Mighty and a Powerful King, and was created next after LUCIFER. He appeareth in the Form of Two Beautiful Angels sitting in a Chariot of Fire. He speaketh with a Comely Voice, and declareth that he fell first from among the worthier sort, that were before Michael, and other Heavenly Angels. His Office is to distribute Presentations and Senatorships, etc.; and to cause favour of Friends and of Foes. He giveth excellent Familiars, and governeth 50 Legions of Spirits. Note well that this King Belial must have Offerings, Sacrifices and Gifts presented unto him by the Exorcist, or else he will not give True Answers unto his Demands. But then he tarrieth not one hour in the Truth, unless he be constrained by Divine Power. And his Seal is this, which is to be worn as aforesaid, etc.

# 69 - DECARABIA

The Sixty-ninth Spirit is Decarabia. He appeareth in the Form of a Star in a Pentacle, at first; but after, at the command of the Exorcist, he putteth on the image of a Man. His Office is to discover the Virtues of Birds and Precious Stones, and to make the Similitude of all kinds of Birds to fly before the Exorcist, singing
and drinking as natural Birds do. He governeth 30
Legions of Spirits, being himself a Great Marquis.
And this is his Seal, which is to be worn, etc.

# 70 - SEERE

The Seventieth Spirit is Seere, Sear, or Seir. He is a Mighty Prince, and Powerful, under AMAYMON, King of the East. He appeareth in the Form of a Beautiful Man, riding upon a Winged Horse. His Office is to go and come; and to bring abundance of things to pass on a sudden, and to carry or recarry anything whither thou wouldest have it to go, or whence thou wouldest have it from. He can pass over the whole Earth in the twinkling of an Eye. He giveth a True relation of all sorts of Theft, and of Treasure hid, and of many other things. He is of an indifferent Good Nature, and is willing to do anything which the Exorcist desireth. He governeth 26 Legions of Spirits. And this his Seal is to be worn, etc.

# 71 - DANTALION

The Seventy-first Spirit is Dantalion. He is a Duke Great and Mighty, appearing in the Form of a Man with many Countenances, all Men's and Women's Faces; and he hath a Book in his right hand. His Office is to teach all Arts and Sciences unto any; and to declare the Secret Counsel of any one; for he knoweth the Thoughts of all Men and Women, and can change them at his Will. He can cause Love, and show the Similitude of any person, and show the same by a Vision, let them be in what part of the World they Will. He governeth 36 Legions of Spirits; and this is his Seal, which wear thou, etc.

# 72 - ANDROMALIUS

The Seventy-second Spirit in Order is named Andromalius. He is an Earl, Great and Mighty, appearing in the Form of a Man holding a Great Serpent in his Hand. His Office is to bring back both a Thief, and the Goods which be stolen; and to discover all Wickedness, and Underhand Dealing; and to punish all Thieves and other Wicked People and also to discover Treasures that be Hid. He ruleth over 36 Legions of Spirits. His Seal is this, the which wear thou as aforesaid, etc.

These be the 72 Mighty Kings and Princes which King Solomon Commanded into a Vessel of Brass, together with their Legions. Of whom BELIAL, BILETH, ASMODAY, and GAAP, were Chief. And it is to be noted that Solomon did this because of their pride, for he never declared other reason why he thus bound them. And when he had thus bound them up and sealed the Vessel, he by Divine Power did chase them all into a deep Lake or Hole in Babylon. And they of Babylon, wondering to see such a thing, they did then go wholly into the Lake, to break the Vessel open, expecting to find great store of Treasure therein. But when they had broken it open, out flew the Chief Spirits immediately, with their Legions following them; and they were all restored to their former places except BELIAL, who entered into a certain Image, and thence gave answers unto those who did offer Sacrifices unto him, and did worship the Image as their God, etc.

## OBSERVATIONS

First, thou shalt know and observe the Moon's Age for thy working. The best days be when the Moon Luna is 2, 4, 6, 8, 10, 12, or 14 days old, as Solomon saith; and no other days be profitable.

The Seals of the 72 Kings are to be made in Metals. The Chief Kings' in Sol (Gold); Marquises' in Luna (Silver); Dukes' in Venus (Copper); Prelacies' in Jupiter (Tin); Knights' in Saturn (Lead); Presidents' in Mercury (Mercury); Earls' in Venus (Copper), and Luna (Silver), alike equal, etc.

THESE 72 Kings be under the Power of AMAYMON, CORSON, ZIMIMAY or ZIMINAIR, and GAAP, who are the Four Great Kings ruling in the Four Quarters, or Cardinal Points, viz.: East, West, North, and South, and are not to be called forth except it be upon Great Occasions; but are to be Invocated and Commanded to send such or such a Spirit that is under their Power and Rule, as is shown in the following Invocations or Conjurations.

And the Chief Kings may be bound from 9 till 12 o'clock at Noon, and from 3 till Sunset; Marquises may be bound from 3 in the afternoon till 9 at Night, and from 9 at Night till Sunrise; Dukes may be bound from Sunrise till Noonday in Clear Weather; Prelates may be bound any hour of the Day; Knights may from Dawning of Day till Sunrise, or from 4 o'clock till Sunset; Presidents may be bound any time, excepting Twilight, at Night, unless the King whom they are under be Invocated; and Counties or Earls any hour of the Day, so it be in Woods, or in any other places whither men resort not, or where no noise is, etc.

# CLASSIFIED LIST OF THE 72 CHIEF SPIRITS OF THE GOETIA, ACCORDING TO RESPECTIVE RANK

*KINGS*, Seal in Gold:

1 - Bael; 9 - Paimon; ; 13 - Beleth; 20 - Purson; 32 - Asmoday; 45 - Vine; 51 - Balam; 61 - Zagan; 68 - Belial.

*DUKES*, Seal in Copper:

2 - Agares; 6 - Valefor; 8 - Barbatos; 11 - Gusion; 15 - Eligos; 16 - Zepar; 18 - Bathim; 19 - Sallos; 23 - Aim; 26 - Bune; 28 - Berith; 29 - Astaroth; 41 - Focalor; 42 - Vepar; 47 - Vual; 49 - Crocell; 52 - Alloces; 54 - Murmur; 56 - Gremory; 60 - Vapula; 64 - Haures; 67 - Amdusias; 71 - Dantalion.

*PRINCES & PRELATES*, Seal in Tin:

3 - Vassago; 12 - Sitri; 22 - Ipos; 33 - Gaap; 36 - Stolas; 55 - Orobas; 70 - Seere.

*MARQUISES*, Seal in Silver:

4 - Samigina; 7 - Amon; 14 - Leraje; 24 - Naberius; 27 - Ronove; 30 - Forneus; 35 - Marchosias; 37 - Phenex; 43 - Sabnock; 44 - Shax; 59 - Orias; 63 - Andras; 65 - Andrealphus; 66 - Cimeies; 69 - Decarabia.

*PRESIDENTS*, Seal in Mercury:

5 - Marbas; 10 - Buer; 17 - Botis; 21 - Marax; 25 - Glasya-Labolas;  31 - Foras; 33 - Gaap; 39 - Malphas; 48 - Haagenti; 53 - Caim;  57 - Ose; 58 - Amy; 61 - Zagan; 62 - Valac.

*EARLS*, or *COUNTS*, Seal in Copper or Silver:

17 - Botis; 21 - Marax; 25 - Glasya-Labolas; 27 - Ronove; 34 - Furfur; 38 - Halphas; 40 - Raum; 45 - Vine; 46 - Bifrons; 72 - Andromalius.

*KNIGHTS*, Seal in Lead:

50 - Furcas.

NOTE: It will be remarked that several among the above Spirits possess two titles of different ranks; e.g., 45 - Vine is both King and Earl; 25 - Glasya-Labolas is both President and Earl, etc. "Prince" and "Prelate" are apparently used as interchangeable terms. Probably the Seals of Earls should be made of Iron, and those of Presidents in mixture either of Copper and Silver, or of Silver and Mercury; as otherwise the Metal of one Planet, Mars, is excluded from the List; the Metals attributed to the Seven Planets being: to Saturn, Lead; to Jupiter, Tin; to Mars, Iron; to the Sun, Gold; to Venus, Copper; to Mercury, Mercury and mixtures of Metals, and to Luna, Silver.

In a manuscript codex by Dr. Rudd, which is in the British Museum, Hebrew names of these 72 Spirits are given; but it appears to me that many are manifestly incorrect in orthography. The codex in question, though beautifully written, also contains many other errors, particularly in the Sigils. Such as they are, these names in the Hebrew of Dr. Rudd are here shown.

## After the Hebrew of Dr. Rudd.

| | | | | | |
|---|---|---|---|---|---|
| 1. Bael<br>כאל<br>Figure 81. | 2. Agares<br>אנגראש<br>Figure 82. | 3. Vassago<br>ושאנו<br>Figure 83. | 4. Gamigin<br>גאמינין<br>Figure 84. | 5. Marbas<br>מארבש<br>Figure 85. | 6. Valefor<br>ואלפאר<br>Figure 86. |
| 7. Amon<br>אמון<br>Figure 87. | 8. Barbatos<br>כרבטוש<br>Figure 88. | 9. Paimon<br>פאימון<br>Figure 89. | 10. Buer<br>בואר<br>Figure 90. | 11. Gusion<br>גוסיון<br>Figure 91. | 12. Sitri<br>שיטרי<br>Figure 92. |
| 13. Beleth<br>כלאת<br>Figure 93. | 14. Leraje<br>לראיך<br>Figure 94. | 15. Eligos<br>אליגוש<br>Figure 95. | 16. Zepar<br>זאפאר<br>Figure 96. | 17. Botis<br>בוטיש<br>Figure 97. | 18. Bathin<br>באתין<br>Figure 98. |
| 19. Sallos<br>שאלוש<br>Figure 99. | 20. Purson<br>פורשון<br>Figure 100. | 21. Marax<br>מאראס<br>Figure 101. | 22. Ipos<br>יפוש<br>Figure 102. | 23. Aim<br>אים<br>Figure 103. | 24. Naberius<br>נבריוש<br>Figure 104. |
| 25. Glasya-Labolas<br>נלאסיא-לב<br>ולש<br>Figure 105. | 26. Bimé<br>ביס<br>Figure 106. | 27. Ronove<br>רונוון<br>Figure 107. | 28. Berith<br>ברית<br>Figure 108. | 29. Astaroth<br>אשטארות<br>Figure 109. | 30. Forneus<br>פהורנאוש<br>Figure 110. |
| 31. Foras<br>פוראש<br>Figure 111. | 32. Asmoday<br>אסמודי<br>Figure 112. | 33. Gaap<br>גאאף<br>Figure 113. | 34. Furfur<br>פהורפהור<br>Figure 114. | 35. Marchosias<br>מרחוסיאש<br>Figure 115. | 36. Stolas<br>שטולוש<br>Figure 116. |
| 37. Phenex<br>פאניס<br>Figure 117. | 38. Malthas<br>מאלתש<br>Figure 118. | 39. Malphas<br>מאלפש<br>Figure 119. | 40. Raum<br>ראום<br>Figure 120. | 41. Focalor<br>פהורכלור<br>Figure 121. | 42. Vepar<br>ופאר<br>Figure 122. |
| 43. Sabnock<br>שבנוך<br>Figure 123. | 44. Shax<br>שאז<br>Figure 124. | 45. Vine<br>וינא<br>Figure 125. | 46. Bifrons<br>ביפהרונש<br>Figure 126. | 47. Uvall<br>וואל<br>Figure 127. | 48. Haagenti<br>האנגטי<br>Figure 128. |
| 49. Crocell<br>כרוכל<br>Figure 129. | 50. Furcas<br>פחדכש<br>Figure 130. | 51. Balam<br>באלאם<br>Figure 131. | 52. Alloces<br>אלוכאס<br>Figure 132. | 53. Camio<br>כאמיו<br>Figure 133. | 54. Murmus<br>מורמוס<br>Figure 134. |
| 55. Orobas<br>ורובש<br>Figure 135. | 56. Gamori<br>נמורי<br>Figure 136. | 57. Voso<br>ושו<br>Figure 137. | 58. Avnas<br>אונש<br>Figure 138. | 59. Oriax<br>וריאס<br>Figure 139. | 60. Naphula<br>נפולא<br>Figure 140. |
| 61. Zagan<br>זאנאן<br>Figure 141. | 62. Valu<br>ואלו<br>Figure 142. | 63. Andras<br>אנדראש<br>Figure 143. | 64. Haures<br>האוראש<br>Figure 144. | 65. Andrealphus<br>אנדראלפהה<br>דיש<br>Figure 145. | 66. Kimaris<br>כימאריש<br>Figure 146. |
| 67. Amdukias<br>אמדוכיאש<br>Figure 147. | 68. Belial<br>בליאל<br>Figure 148. | 69. Decarabia<br>דכארביא<br>Figure 149. | 70. Seere<br>שאר<br>Figure 150. | 71. Dantalion<br>דאנטאליון<br>Figure 151. | 72. Andromalius<br>אנדרומלידיש<br>Figure 152. |

# THE MAGICAL CIRCLE

This is the Form of the Magical Circle of King Solomon (Fig.153), the which he made that he might preserve himself therein from the malice of these Evil Spirits.

This Magical Circle is to be made 9 feet across, and the Divine Names are to be written around it, beginning at EHYEH, and ending at LEVANAH, Luna.

*COLOURS:*

The space between the outer and inner circles, where the serpent is coiled, with the Hebrew names written along his body, is bright deep yellow.

The square in the centre of the circle, where the word "Master" is written, is filled in with red. All names and letters are in black.

In the Hexagrams the outer triangles where the letters A, D, O, N, A, I, appear are filled in with bright yellow, the centres, where the T-shaped crosses are, blue or green.

In the Pentagrams outside the circle, the outer triangles where "Te, tra, gram, ma, ton," is written, are filled in bright yellow, and the centres with the T crosses written therein are red.")

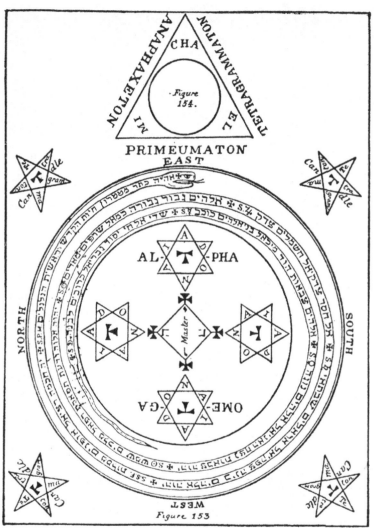

*The coiled serpent is only shown in one private codex, the Hebrew names being in most cases simply written round in a somewhat spiral arrangement within the double circle. It is to be remembered that Hebrew is always written from right to left, instead of from left to right like ordinary European languages. The small Maltese crosses are placed to mark the conclusion of each separate set of Hebrew names. These names are those of Deity Angels and Archangels allotted by the Qabalists to each of the 9 first Sephiroth or Divine Emanations. In English letters they run thus, beginning from the head of the serpent: + Ehyeh Kether Metatron Chaioth Ha-Qadehs Rashith Ha-Galgalim S.P.M. (for "Sphere of the Primum Mobile") + Iah Chokmah Ratziel Auphanim Masloth S.S.F (for "Sphere of the Fixed Stars," or S.Z. for "Sphere of the Zodiac") + Iehovah Eolhim Binah Tzaphquiel Aralim Shabbathai S. (for "Sphere") of Saturn + El Chesed Tzadquiel Chaschmalim Tzedeq S. of Jupiter + Elohim Gibor Geburah Kamael Seraphim Madim S. of Mars + Iehovah Eloah Va-Daath Tiphereth Raphael Malakim Shemesh S. of the Sun + Iehovah Tzabaoth Netzach Haniel Elohim Nogah S. of Venus. + Elohim Tzabaoth Hod Michael Beni Elohim Kokav S. of Mercury + Shaddai El Chai Iesod Gabriel Cherubim Levanah S. of the Moon +*

# THE MAGICAL TRIANGLE

This is the Form of the Magical Triangle (Fig.154), into the which Solomon did command the Evil Spirits.

It is to be made at 2 feet distance from the Magical Circle and it is 3 feet across. Note that this triangle is to be placed toward that quarter whereunto the Spirit belongeth.

And the base of the triangle is to be nearest unto the Circle, the apex pointing in the direction of the quarter of the Spirit.

Observe thou also the Moon in thy working, as aforesaid, etc. Anaphaxeton is sometimes written Anepheneton.


*COLOURS*:

Triangle outlined in black; name of Michael black on white ground; the three Names without the triangle written in red; circle in centre entirely filled in in dark green.

# THE HEXAGRAM

This is the Form of the Hexagram of Solomon, the figure whereof is to be made on parchment of a calf's skin, and worn at the skirt of thy white vestment, and covered with a cloth of fine linen white and pure, the which is to be shown unto the Spirits when they do appear, so that they be compelled to take human shape upon them and be obedient.

*COLOURS:*

Circle, Hexagon, and T cross in centre outlined in black, Maltese crosses black; the five exterior triangles of the Hexagram where Te, tra, gram, ma, ton, is written, are filled in with bright yellow; the T cross in centre is red, with the three little squares therein in black. The lower exterior triangle, where the Sigil is drawn in black, is left white. The words " Tetragrammaton" and "Tau" are in black letters; and AGLA with Alpha and Omega in red letters.

# THE PENTAGRAM

This is the Form of Pentagram of Solomon, the figure whereof is to be made in Sol or Luna (Gold or Silver), and worn upon thy breast; having the Seal of the Spirit required upon the other side thereof. It is to preserve thee from danger, and also to command the Spirits by.

*COLOURS*:

Circle and pentagram outlined in black. Names and Sigils within Pentagram black also. "Tetragrammaton" in red letters. Ground of centre of Pentagram, where "Soluzen" is written, green. External angles of Pentagram where "Abdia ... .. Ballaton, Halliza, " etc., are written, blue.

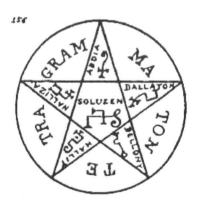

# THE MAGIC RING

This is the Form of the Magic Ring, or rather Disc, of Solomon, the figure whereof is to be made in gold or silver. It is to be held before the face of the exorcist to preserve him from the stinking sulphurous fumes and flaming breath of the Evil Spirits.

*COLOURS:*

Bright yellow. Letters, black.

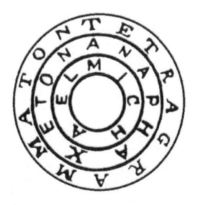

# THE VESSEL OF BRASS

This is the Form of the Vessel of Brass (Fig.158;Fig.159) wherein King Solomon did shut up the Evil Spirits, etc.

Somewhat different forms are given in the various codices. The seal in the next page was made in brass to cover this vessel with at the top. This history of the genii shut up in the brazen vessel by King Solomon recalls the story of "The Fisherman and the Jinni " in "The Arabian Nights." In this tale, however, there was only one jinni shut up in a vessel of yellow brass the which was covered at the top with a leaden seal. This jinni tells the fisherman that his name is Sakhr, or Sacar.


COLOURS:

Bronze. Letters: Black on a red band.

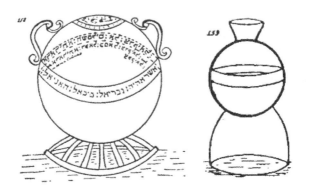

# THE SECRET SEAL

This is the Form of the Secret Seal of Solomon, wherewith he did bind and seal up the aforesaid Spirits with their legions in the Vessel of Brass.

This seal is to be made by one that is clean both inwardly and outwardly, and that hath not defiled himself by any woman in the space of a month, but hath in prayer and fasting desired of God to forgive him all his sins, etc.

It is to be made on the day of Mars or Saturn (Tuesday or Saturday) at night at 12 o'clock, and written upon virgin parchment with the blood of a black cock that never trode hen. Note that on this night the moon must be increasing in light (i.e., going from new to full) and in the Zodiacal Sign of Virgo. And when the seal is so made thou shalt perfume it with alum, raisins dried in the sun, dates, cedar and lignum aloes.

Also, by this seal King Solomon did command all the aforesaid Spirits in the Vessel of Brass, and did seal it up with this same seal. He by it gained the love of all manner of persons, and overcame in battle, for neither weapons, nor fire, nor water could hurt him. And this privy seal was made to cover the vessel at the top withal, etc.

# THE OTHER MAGICAL REQUISITES

The other magical requisites are: a sceptre, a sword, a mitre, a cap, a long white robe of linen, and other garments for the purpose (in many Codices it is written "a sceptre or sword, a mitre or cap." By the "other garments" would be meant not only undergarments, but, also mantles of different colours) ; also a girdle of lion's skin three inches broad, with all the names written about it which be round the outmost part of the Magical Circle.

Also perfumes, and a chafing-dish of charcoal kindled to put the fumes on, to smoke or perfume the place appointed for action; also anointing oil to anoint thy temples and thine eyes with; and fair water to wash thyself in.

And in so doing, thou shalt say as David said:

*"Thou shalt purge me with hyssop, O Lord! and I shall be clean: Thou shalt wash me, and I shall be whiter than snow. "*

And at the putting on of thy garments thou shalt say:

*"By the figurative mystery of these holy vestures (or of this holy vestment) I will clothe me with the armour of salvation in the strength of the Most High, ANCHOR; AMACOR; AMIDES; THEODINIAS; ANITOR; that my desired end may be effected through Thy strength, O ADONAI! unto Whom the praise and glory will for ever and ever belong! Amen!"*

After thou hast so done, make prayers unto God according unto thy work, as Solomon hath commanded.

# THE CONJURATION TO CALL FORTH
# ANY OF THE AFORESAID SPIRITS

*"I invocate and conjure thee, O Spirit, (NAME OF THE SPIRIT); and being with power armed from the SUPREME MAJESTY, I do strongly command thee, by BERALANENSIS, BALDA-CHIENSIS, PAUMACHIA, and APOLOGIAE SEDES; by the most Powerful Princes, Genii, Liachidee, and Ministers of the Tartarean Abode; and by the Chief Prince of the Seat of Apologia in the Ninth Legion, I do invoke thee, and by invocating conjure thee. And being armed with power from the SUPREME MAJESTY, I do strongly command thee, by Him Who spake and it was done, and unto whom all creatures be obedient. Also I, being made after the image of GOD, endued with power from GOD and created according unto His will, do exorcise thee by that most mighty and powerful name of GOD, EL, strong and wonderful; O thou Spirit N. And I command thee and Him who spake the Word and His FIAT was accomplished, and by all the names of God. Also by the names ADONAI, EL, ELOHIM, ELOHI, EHYEH, ASHER EHYEH, ZABAOTH, ELION, IAH, TETRAGRAMMATON, SHADDAI, LORD GOD MOST HIGH, I do exorcise thee and do powerfully command thee, O thou Spirit N., that thou dost forthwith appear unto me here before this Circle in a fair human shape, without any deformity or tortuosity. And by this ineffable name, TETRAGRAMMATON IEHOVAH, do I command thee, at the which being heard the elements are overthrown, the air is shaken, the sea runneth back, the fire is quenched, the earth trembleth, and all the hosts of the celestials, terrestrials, and infernals, do tremble together, and are troubled and confounded. Wherefore come thou, O Spirit N., forthwith, and without delay, from any or all parts of the world wherever thou mayest be, and make rational answers unto all things that I shall demand of thee. Come thou peaceably, visibly, and affably, now, and without delay, manifesting that which I shall desire. For thou art conjured by the name of the LIVING and TRUE GOD, HELIOREN, wherefore fulfil thou my commands, and persist thou therein unto the end, and according unto mine interest, visibly and affably speaking unto me with a voice clear and intelligible without any ambiguity."*

Repeat this conjuration as often as thou pleasest, and if the Spirit come not yet, say as followeth:

## THE SECOND CONJURATION

*"I DO invoke, conjure, and command thee, O thou Spirit N., to appear and to show thyself visibly unto me before this Circle in fair and comely shape, without any deformity or tortuosity; by the name and in the name IAH and VAU, which Adam heard and spake; and by the name of GOD, AGLA, which Lot heard and was saved with his family; and by the name IOTH, which Jacob heard from the angel wrestling with him, and was delivered from the hand of Esau his brother; and by the name ANAPHAXETON which Aaron heard and spake and was made wise; and by the name ZABAOTH, which Moses named and all the rivers were turned into blood; and by the name ASHER EHYEH ORISTON, which Moses named, and all the rivers brought forth frogs, and they ascended into the houses, destroying all things; and by the name ELION, which Moses named, and there was great hail such as had not been since the beginning Of the world; and by the name ADONAI, which Moses named, and there came up locusts, which appeared upon the whole land, and devoured all which the hail had left; and by the name SCHEMA AMATHIA which Ioshua called upon, and the sun stayed his course; and by the name ALPHA and OMEGA, which Daniel named, and destroyed Bel, and slew the Dragon; and in the name EMMANUEL, which the three children, Shadrach, Meshach and Abed-nego, sang in the midst of the fiery furnace, and were delivered; and by the name HAGIOS; and by the SEAL31 OF ADONI; and by ISCHYROS, ATHANATOS, PARACLETOS; and by O THEOS, ICTROS, ATHANATOS; and by these three secret names, AGLA, ON, TETRAGRAMMATON, do I adjure and constrain thee. And by these names, and by all the other names of the LIVING and TRUE GOD, the LORD ALMIGHTY, I do exorcise and command thee, O Spirit N., even by Him Who spake the Word and it was done, and to Whom all creatures are obedient; and by the dreadful judgments of GOD; and by the uncertain Sea of Glass, which is before the DIVINE MAJESTY, mighty and powerful; by the four beasts before the throne, having eyes before and behind; by the fire round about the throne; by the holy*

*angels of Heaven; and by the mighty wisdom of GOD; I do potently exorcise thee, that thou appearest here before this Circle, to fulfil my will in all things which shall seem good unto me; by the Seal of BASDATHEA BALDA-CHIA; and by this name PRIMEUMATON, which Moses named, and the earth opened, and did swallow up Kora, Dathan, and Abiram. Wherefore thou shalt make faithful answers unto all my demands, O Spirit N., and shalt perform all my desires so far as in thine office thou art capable hereof. Wherefore, come thou, visibly, peaceably, and affably, now without delay, to manifest that which I desire, speaking with a clear and perfect voice, intelligibly, and to mine understanding."*

If he come not yet at the rehearsal of these two first conjurations (but without doubt he will), say on as followeth; it being a constraint:

## THE CONSTRAINT

*"I DO conjure thee, O thou Spirit N., by all the most glorious and efficacious names of the MOST GREAT AND INCOMPREHENSIBLE LORD GOD OF HOSTS, that thou comest quickly and without delay from all parts and places of the earth and world wherever thou mayest be, to make rational answers unto my demands, and that visibly and affably, speaking with a voice intelligible unto mine understanding as aforesaid. I conjure and constrain thee, O thou Spirit N., by all the names aforesaid; and in addition by these seven great names wherewith Solomon the Wise bound thee and thy companions in a Vessel of Brass, ADONAI, PREYAI or PRERAI, TETRAGRAMMATON, ANAPHAXETON or ANEPHENETON, INESSENFATOAL or INESSENFATALL, PATHTUMON or PATHATUMON, and ITEMON; that thou appearest here before this Circle to fulfil my will in all things that seem good unto me. And if thou be still so disobedient, and refusest still to come, I will in the power and by the power of the name of the SUPREME AND EVERLASTING LORD GOD WHO created both thee and me and all the world in six days, and what is contained therein, EIE, SARAYE, and by the power of this name PRIMEUMATON which commandeth the whole host of Heaven, curse thee, and deprive thee of thine office, joy, and*

*place, and bind thee in the depths of the Bottomless Pit or Abyss, there to remain unto the Day of the Last Judgment. And I will bind thee in the Eternal Fire, and into the Lake of Flame and of Brimstone, unless thou comest quickly and appearest here before this Circle to do my will. Therefore, come thou! in and by the holy names ADONAI, ZABAOTH, ADONAI, AMIORAN. Come thou! for it is ADONAI who commandest thee."*

If thou hast come thus far, and yet he appeareth not, thou mayest be sure that he is sent unto some other place by his King, and cannot come; and if it be so, invocate the King as here followeth, to send him. But if he do not come still, then thou mayest be sure that he is bound in chains in hell, and that he is not in the custody of his King. If so, and thou still hast a desire to call him even from thence, thou must rehearse the general curse which is called the Spirits' Chain.

Here followeth, therefore, the Invocation of the King:

## THE INVOCATION OF THE KING

*"O thou great, powerful, and mighty KING AMAIMON, who bearest rule by the power of the SUPREME GOD EL over all spirits both superior and inferior of the Infernal Orders in the Dominion of the East; I do invocate and command thee by the especial and true name of GOD; and by that God that Thou Worshippest; and by the Seal of thy creation; and by the most mighty and powerful name of GOD, IEHOVAH TETRAGRAMMATON who cast thee out of heaven with all other infernal spirits; and by all the most powerful and great names of GOD who created Heaven, and Earth, and Hell, and all things in them contained; and by their power and virtue; and by the name PRIMEUMATON who commandeth the whole host of Heaven; that thou mayest cause, enforce, and compel the Spirit N. to come unto me here before this Circle in a fair and comely shape, without harm unto me or unto any other creature, to answer truly and faithfully unto all my requests; so that I may accomplish my will and desire in knowing or obtaining*

*any matter or thing which by office thou knowest is proper for him to perform or accomplish, through the power of GOD, EL, Who created and doth dispose of all things both celestial, aerial terrestrial, and infernal."*

AFTER thou shalt have invocated the King in this manner twice or thrice over, then conjure the spirit thou wouldst call forth by the aforesaid conjurations, rehearsing them several times together, and he will come without doubt, if not at the first or second time of rehearsing.

But if he do not come, add the "Spirits' Chain" unto the end of the aforesaid conjurations, and he will be forced to come, even if he be bound in chains, for the chains must break off from him, and he will be at liberty:

## THE GENERAL CURSE, CALLED THE SPIRITS' CHAIN, AGAINST ALL SPIRITS THAT REBEL

*"O THOU wicked and disobedient spirit N., because thou hast rebelled, and hast not obeyed nor regarded my words which I have rehearsed; they being all glorious and incomprehensible names of the true GOD, the maker and creator of thee and of me, and of all the world; I DO by the power of these names the which no creature is able to resist, curse thee into the depth of the Bottomless Abyss, there to remain unto the Day of Doom in chains, and in fire and brimstone unquenchable, unless thou forthwith appear here before this Circle, in this triangle to do my will. And, therefore, come thou quickly and peaceably, in and by these Dames of GOD, ADONAI, ZABAOTH, ADONAI, AMIORAN; come thou! come thou! for it is the King of Kings, even ADONAI, who commandeth thee."*

When thou shalt have rehearsed thus far, but still be cometh not, then write thou his seal on parchment and put thou it into a strong black box; with brimstone, asafetida and such like things that bear a stinking smell; and then bind the box up round with an iron wire, and hang it upon the point of thy sword, and hold it over the fire of charcoal; and say as followeth unto the fire first, it being placed toward that quarter whence the Spirit is to come:

## THE CONJURATION OF THE FIRE

*"I conjure thee, O fire, by him who made thee and all other creatures for good in the world, that thou torment, burn, and consume this Spirit N., for everlasting. I condemn thee, thou Spirit N., because thou art disobedient and obeyest not my commandment, nor keepest the precepts of the LORD Thy GOD, neither wilt thou obey me nor mine invocations, having thereby called thee forth, I, who am the servant of the MOST HIGH AND IMPERIAL LORD GOD OF HOSTS, IEHOVAH, I who am dignified and fortified by His celestial power and permission, and yet thou comest not to answer these my propositions here made unto thee. For the which thine averseness and contempt thou art guilty of great disobedience and rebellion, and therefore shall I excommunicate thee, and destroy thy name and seal, the which I have enclosed in this box; and shall burn thee in the immortal fire and bury thee in immortal oblivion; unless thou immediately come and appear visibly and affably, friendly and courteously here unto me before this Circle, in this triangle, in a form comely and fair, and in no wise terrible, hurtful, or frightful to me or any other creature whatsoever upon the face of earth. And thou shalt make rational answers unto my requests, and perform all my desires in all things, that I shall make unto thee."*

And if he come not even yet, thou shalt say as followeth:

# THE CURSE

*"Now O thou Spirit N., since thou art still pernicious and disobedient, and wilt not appear unto me to answer unto such things as I would have desired of thee, or would have been satisfied in; I do in the name, and by the power and dignity of the Omnipresent and Immortal Lord God of Hosts IEHOVAH TETRAGRAMMATON, the only creator of Heaven, and Earth, and Hell, and all that is therein, who is the marvellous Disposer of all things both visible and invisible, curse thee, and deprive thee of all thine office, joy, and place; and I do bind thee in the depths of the Bottomless Abyss there to remain until the Day of Judgment, I say into the Lake of Fire and Brimstone which is prepared for all rebellious, disobedient, obstinate, and pernicious spirits. Let all the company of Heaven curse thee! Let the sun, moon, and all the stars curse thee! Let the LIGHT and all the hosts of Heaven curse thee into the fire unquenchable, and into the torments unspeakable. And as thy name and seal contained in this box chained and bound up, shall be choken in sulphurous stinking substances, and burned in this material fire; so in the name IEHOVAH and by the power and dignity of these three names, TETRAGRAMMATON, ANAPHAXETON, and PRIMEUMATON, I do cast thee, O thou wicked and disobedient Spirit N., into the Lake of Fire which is prepared for the damned and accursed spirits, and there to remain unto the day of doom, and never more to be remembered before the face of GOD, who shall come to judge the quick, and the dead, and the world, by fire."*

Then the exorcist must put the box into the fire, and by-and-by the Spirit will come, but as soon as he is come, quench the fire that the box is in, and make a sweet perfume, and give him welcome and a kind entertainment, showing unto him the Pentacle that is at the bottom of your vesture covered with a linen cloth, saying:

# THE ADDRESS UNTO THE SPIRIT
## UPON HIS COMING

*"BEHOLD thy confusion if thou refusest to be obedient! Behold the Pentacle of Solomon which I have brought here before thy presence! Behold the person of the exorcist in the midst of the exorcism; him who is armed by GOD and without fear; him who potently invocateth thee and calleth thee forth unto appearance; even him, thy master, who is called OCTINIMOS. Wherefore make rational answer unto my demands, and prepare to be obedient unto thy master in the name of the Lord:*

> *BATHAL VEL VATHAT SUPER ABRAE RUENS!*
> *ABEOR VENIENS SUPER ABERER!"*

Then he or they will be obedient, and bid thee ask what thou wilt, for he or they be subjected by God to fulfil our desires and commands. And when he or they shall have appeared and showed himself or themselves humble and meek, then shalt thou rehearse:

# THE WELCOME UNTO THE SPIRIT

*"Welcome Spirit N., O most noble king36 (or kings)! I say thou art welcome unto me, because I have called thee through Him who has created Heaven, and Earth, and Hell, and all that is in them contained, and because also thou hast obeyed. By that same power by the which I have called thee forth, I bind thee, that thou remain affably and visibly here before this Circle (or before this Circle and in this triangle) so constant and so long as I shall have occasion for thy presence; and not to depart without my license until thou hast duly and faithfully performed my will without any falsity."*

THEN standing in the midst of the Circle, thou shall stretch forth thine hand in a gesture of command and say:

*"BY THE PENTACLE OF SOLOMON HAVE I CALLED THEE! GIVE UNTO ME A TRUE ANSWER!"*

Then let the exorcist state his desires and requests.

And when the evocation is finished thou shalt license the Spirit to depart thus:

## THE LICENSE TO DEPART

*"O thou Spirit N., because thou hast diligently answered unto my demands, and hast been very ready and willing to come at my call, I do here license thee to depart unto thy proper place; without causing harm or danger unto man or beast. Depart, then, I say, and be thou very ready to come at my call, being duly exorcised and conjured by the sacred rites of magic. I charge thee to withdraw peaceably and quietly and the peace of god be ever continued between thee and me! AMEN"*

After thou hast given the Spirit license to depart, thou art not to go out of the circle until he or they be gone, and until thou shalt have made prayers and rendered thanks unto God for the great blessings He hath bestowed upon thee in granting thy desires, and delivering thee from all the malice of the enemy the devil.

Also note! Thou mayest command these spirits into the Vessel of Brass in the same manner as thou dost into the triangle, by saying:

*"that thou dost forthwith appear before this Circle, in this Vessel of Brass, in a fair and comely shape,"* etc.

as hath been shown in the foregoing conjurations.

*HERE ENDETH THIS FIRST BOOK OF
THE LEMEGETON, WHICH IS CALLED*

*THE GOETIA.*

THE   LESSER   KEY   OF   SOLOMON

# LEMEGETON

BOOK II, ARS THEURGIA GOETIA

SOURCE MATERIAL

*VARIOUS SOURCES & MANUSCRIPTS*

# HERE BEGINNETH THE SECOND BOOK, CALLED THE

# ARS THEURGIA GOETIA

# OF SOLOMON THE KING

In this following treatise you have the names of the Chief Spirits with several of the Ministring Spirits that are under them, with their Seals or charactors which are to be worn as a Lamen on your breast, for without that the Spirit that has appeared will not obey to do your will.

The office of these Spirits is all one, for what one can do the others can do the same, they can show & discover all things that are hidden, and done in the world & can fetch & carry & do any thing that is to be done or contained in any of the 4 Elements, Fire, Air, Earth or Water, & also the secrets of Kings or any other persons or person, let it be in what kind it will.

These are by nature good & evil, that is the one part is good & the other part is Evil, they are governed by their Princes, & each Prince hath his abode in the points of the Compass, as is showed in the following figure, therefore when you have a desire to call any of the Princes or any of their servants, you are to direct your self towards that point of the Compass the King or Prince has his mansion or place of Abode, & you cannot well err in your operations, note every Prince is to have his Conjuration, yet all of one form, excepting the name and place of the Spirit for in that they must change & differ, also the seals of the Spirits are to be changed accordingly.

As for the garments & other materials, they are spoken of in the Book Goetia, aforesaid.

The Forme of the figure which Discovers the orders of the 31 Kings or Princes with their Servants & Ministers, for when the King is found his subjects are easy to be found out.

The Figure Followeth:

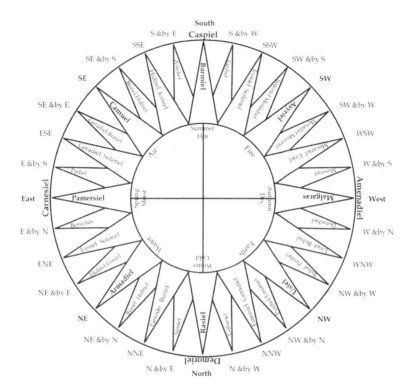

You may perceive by this figure that 20 of these Kings have then fixed mansions & continue in one place, & the others are movable & are sometimes in one place & sometimes another & sometimes in another more or less.

Therefore it is no matter which way you stand with your face when you desire to call them or their servants. Carnesiel is the most chief & great Emperor ruling the East, who hath 1000 great Dukes & 100 Lessor Dukes under him, besides 500,000,000,000 of ministring Spirits which are more inferior than the Dukes, whereof we shall make no mention but only 12 of the chief Dukes & their seals because they are sufficient for practise.

THE   SPIRITS   OF   THE

# ARS THEURGIA
# GOETIA

# 1 - CARNESIEL

When you call Carnesiel either by day or by night, there Attend him 60,000,000,000,000 Dukes, but when you call any of his Dukes, there never Attends above 300 & sometimes not above 10.

The Conjuration:

*"I conjure thee O thou great mighty & potent Prince Carnesiel, &c."*

The full conjurations are at the end of the book.

## THE SEALS OF HIS 12 DUKES:

1 - ORVICH

2 - BENOHAM

3 - VADRIEL

4 - BEDARY

5 - ZABRIEL

6 - ARIFEL

7 - ARMANY

8 - MYREZYN

9 - BUCAFAS

10 - CUMERZEL

11 - CAPRIEL

12 - LAPHOR

# 2 - CASPIEL

Caspiel is the Chiefest Emperor Ruling the South who hath 200 great Dukes & 400 lesser Dukes under him besides 1,000,200,000,000 of Ministring Spirits which are much inferior & whereof we shall make no mention but only of these 12 being the chief Dukes & their seals for they are sufficient for practise.

Each of these 12 Dukes have 2660 under Dukes apeace to Attend them, whereof some of them come along with him when he is invocated but they are very stubborn & churlish.

The Conjuration:

*"I Conjure thee O thou Mighty & Potent Prince Caspiel, &c."*

## THE SEALS OF HIS 12 DUKES:

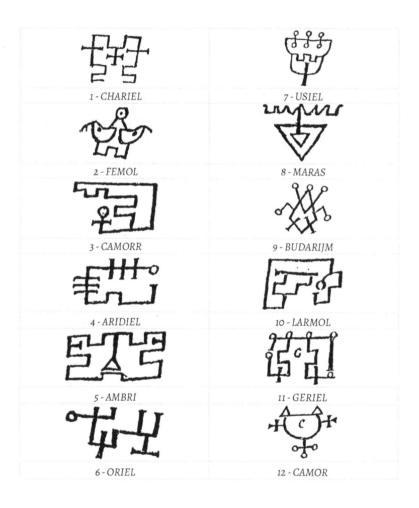

| | |
|---|---|
| 1 - CHARIEL | 7 - USIEL |
| 2 - FEMOL | 8 - MARAS |
| 3 - CAMORR | 9 - BUDARIJM |
| 4 - ARIDIEL | 10 - LARMOL |
| 5 - AMBRI | 11 - GERIEL |
| 6 - ORIEL | 12 - CAMOR |

# 3 - AMENADIEL

Amenadiel is the great Emperor of the West who hath 300 great Dukes & 500 lesser Dukes besides 40,000,030,000,100,000 other ministring Spirits more inferior to Attend him, whereof we shall not make any mention but only 12 of the Chief Dukes & their seals which is sufficient for practice.

The Conjuration:

*"I conjure thee O thou great & mighty & potent prince Amenadiel, who is the Emperor & chief King ruling in the Dominion of the West, &c "*

## THE SEALS OF HIS 12 DUKES:

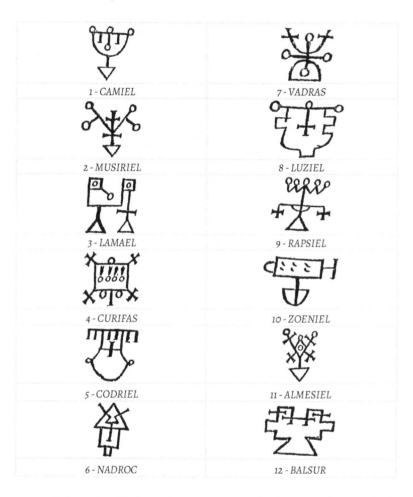

| | |
|---|---|
| 1 - CAMIEL | 7 - VADRAS |
| 2 - MUSIRIEL | 8 - LUZIEL |
| 3 - LAMAEL | 9 - RAPSIEL |
| 4 - CURIFAS | 10 - ZOENIEL |
| 5 - CODRIEL | 11 - ALMESIEL |
| 6 - NADROC | 12 - BALSUR |

Amenadiel may be called any time the day or night, but his Dukes who hath 3000 servants a piece to attend them are to be called in certain hours, as Vadras he may be called in the 2 first hours of the day, and so successively till you come to Nadroc who is to be called in the 2 last hours of the night, & then begins again (with) Vadras &c. The same rule is to be observed calling the Dukes belonging to Demoriel the Emperor of the North.

# 4 - DEMORIEL

Demoriel is the great & mighty Emperor of the North, who hath 400 Great Dukes & 600 lesser Dukes with 700,000,800,000,000,000 servants under his command to Attend him, whereof we shall make no mention but of 12 of the Chief Dukes & their seals which is sufficient for practise.

Each of these Dukes hath 1140 servants who Attend them as need requireth, for when the Duke is called for, & you have more to do than ordinary, he hath more servants to Attend him.

The Conjuration:

"*I Conjure thee O thou great & mighty & Potent Prince Demoriel, &c.*"

## THE SEALS OF HIS 12 DUKES:

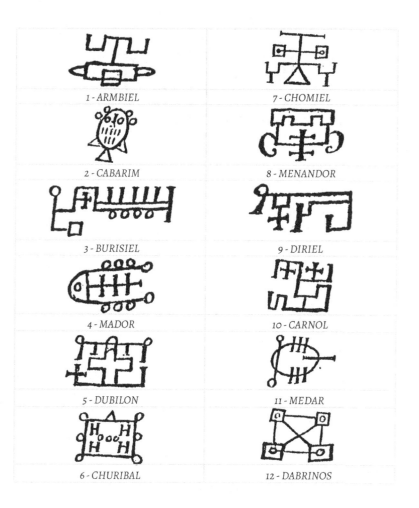

1 - ARMBIEL

2 - CABARIM

3 - BURISIEL

4 - MADOR

5 - DUBILON

6 - CHURIBAL

7 - CHOMIEL

8 - MENANDOR

9 - DIRIEL

10 - CARNOL

11 - MEDAR

12 - DABRINOS

# 5 - PAMERSIEL

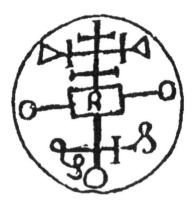

Pamersiel is the first & chief Spirit ruling in the East under Canesiel who hath a thousand Spirits under him, none is to be called in the daytime but with great care for they are very lofty & stubborn, whereof we shall make mention of 11.

These Spirits are by nature Evil & very false & not to be trusted in Secrets but are excellent in driving away Spirits of Darkness from anything that is haunted such as houses, & to call forth Pamersiel or any of these his servants, make a circle in the form as is showed in the Book I Goetia before going in the upper room of your house, or in a place that is Airy because these Spirits that are in this part are all Airy. You may call these Spirits into a Crystal Stone 4 inches in Diameter sett on a table made as followeth which is called the Secret Table of Solomon, having his seal on your breast & the girdle about your waist, as is showed in the Book Goetia, and you cannot err. The form of the table is this, when you have thus got what is to be prepared, rehearse the Conjuration following several times, that is whilst the Spirit comes, for without a doubt he will come.

The Conjuration:

*"I conjure thee, O thou mighty & potent Prince Pamersiel who Ruleth as a King in the Dominion of the East, &c."*

NOTE: THE SAME METHOD IS USED IN ALL THE FOLLOWING SPIRITS OF THIS BOOK II THEURGIA GOETIA, AS IS HERE OF PAMERSIEL & HIS SERVANTS AFORESAID.

# THE SEALS OF HIS 11 SERVANTS:

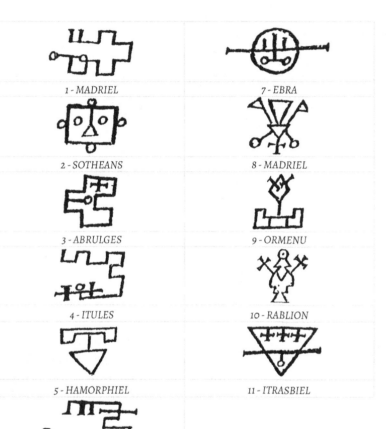

| | |
|---|---|
| 1 - MADRIEL | 7 - EBRA |
| 2 - SOTHEANS | 8 - MADRIEL |
| 3 - ABRULGES | 9 - ORMENU |
| 4 - ITULES | 10 - RABLION |
| 5 - HAMORPHIEL | 11 - ITRASBIEL |
| 6 - ANOYR | |

SOLOMON'S TABLE

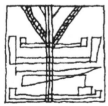

# 6 - PADIEL

The 2nd. Spirit in order under the Empire of the East, is Padiel, he Ruleth in the East & By South as a King & Governeth 10,000 Spirits by day & 200,000 by night besides several thousand under them, they are all naturally good & may be trusted, Solomon saith those Spirits hath no power of themselves but what is given them by their Prince Padiel, therefore he hath made no mention of any of their names, because if any of them be called they cannot appear without the leave of Prince Padiel, as is declared before Pamersiel.

The Conjuration:

*"I Conjure thee O thou mighty & Potent prince Padiel, who rules as chief prince in the Dominion or the East & By south, &c ".*

# 7 - CAMUEL

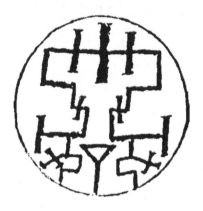

The third Spirit in Order which is under the Chief King of the East is Camuel, who ruleth as a King in the South East part of the World, who hath several Spirits under his command whereas we shall make mention of 10 that belong to the Day & as many that belong to the Night, & each of these have 10 servants to attend them, excepting Camyel, Citgaras, Calym, Meras, for they have 100 apiece to attend them, but Tediol, Moriol & Tugaros, they have none at all.

They appear all in a very beautiful form & very courteously in the Night as well as the Day, and they are as followeth with their Seals.

The Conjuration:

*"I Conjure thee O thou mighty & Potent Prince, &c."*

## THE SEALS OF CAMUEL'S 10 SERVANTS BELONGING TO THE DAY:

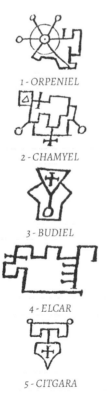

1 - ORPENIEL

2 - CHAMYEL

3 - BUDIEL

4 - ELCAR

5 - CITGARA

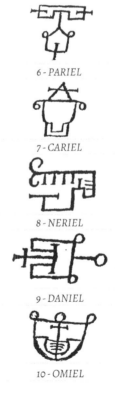

6 - PARIEL

7 - CARIEL

8 - NERIEL

9 - DANIEL

10 - OMIEL

# THE SEALS OF CAMUEL'S 10 SERVANTS BELONGING TO THE NIGHT:

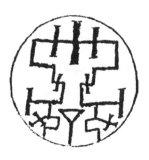

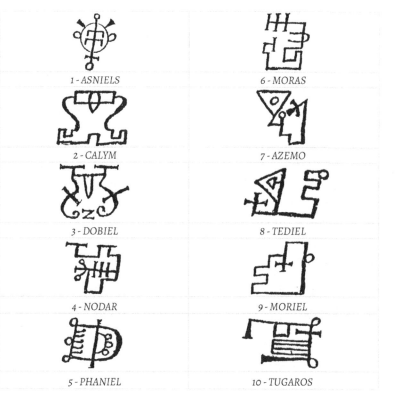

| | |
|---|---|
| 1 - ASNIELS | 6 - MORAS |
| 2 - CALYM | 7 - AZEMO |
| 3 - DOBIEL | 8 - TEDIEL |
| 4 - NODAR | 9 - MORIEL |
| 5 - PHANIEL | 10 - TUGAROS |

# 8 - ASTELIEL

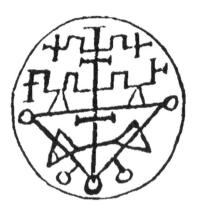

The 4th Spirit in order is Asteliel, he governeth as King under Carnesiel in the South & by East, be hath 10 chief Spirits belonging to the Day & 20 to the Night, under whom are 3 principal Spirits & under these as many, whereof we shall make mention of 8 of the chief presidents belonging to the Day & as many to the Night, every one hath 20 servants at his command, they are all very courteous & loving & beautiful to behold & they are as followeth with there their seals.

The Conjuration:

*"I conjure thee O thou Mighty & Potent Prince Asteliel &c."*

Those Spirits which belong to the Night are to be called in the Night, & those of the Day in the Day.

# THE SEALS OF ASTELIEL'S 8 PRESIDENTS BELONGING TO THE DAY:

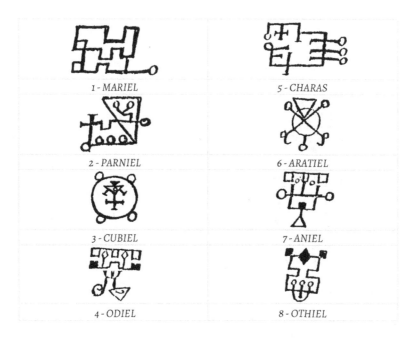

| | |
|---|---|
| 1 - MARIEL | 5 - CHARAS |
| 2 - PARNIEL | 6 - ARATIEL |
| 3 - CUBIEL | 7 - ANIEL |
| 4 - ODIEL | 8 - OTHIEL |

# THE SEALS OF ASTELIEL'S 8 PRESIDENTS BELONGING TO THE NIGHT:

1 - SARIEL

2 - AREAM

3 - CHAMOS

4 - BUFAR

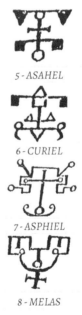

5 - ASAHEL

6 - CURIEL

7 - ASPHIEL

8 - MELAS

# 9 - BARMIEL

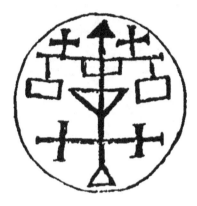

The 5th. Spirit in order is Barmiel, he is the first & chief Spirit under Caspiel, the Emperor of the South, he governs as King under Caspiel & hath 10 Dukes for the Day & 20 for the Night to attend him to do his will, the which are all very good & willing to obey the Exorcist, whereof we shall make mention but of 8 that belong to the day & as many for the night, with their seals for they are sufficient for practise.

Every one of these Dukes hath 20 servants apeace to Attend them when they are called, excepting the last 4 that belong to the night, for they have none.

The Conjuration:


*"I conjure thee O thou mighty & Potent Prince Barmiel, &c."*


Those Spirits which belong to the Night are to be called in the Night, & those of the Day in the Day.

## THE SEALS OF BARMIEL'S 8 DUKES BELONGING TO THE DAY:

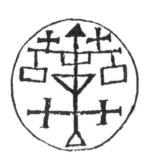

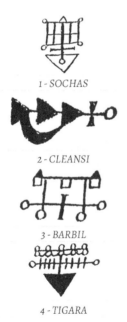

1 - SOCHAS

2 - CLEANSI

3 - BARBIL

4 - TIGARA

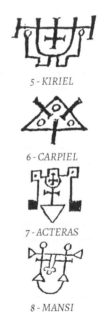

5 - KIRIEL

6 - CARPIEL

7 - ACTERAS

8 - MANSI

# THE SEALS OF BARMIEL'S 8 DUKES BELONGING TO THE NIGHT:

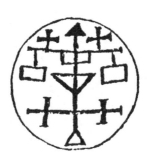

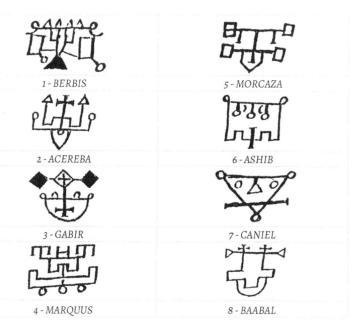

1 - BERBIS

5 - MORCAZA

2 - ACEREBA

6 - ASHIB

3 - GABIR

7 - CANIEL

4 - MARQUUS

8 - BAABAL

# 10 - GEDIEL

The 6th. Spirit in order, but the second under the Empire of the South is Gediel, who ruleth as King in the South & by West, who hath 20 chief Spirits to serve him in the Day & as many in the Night, & they have servants at their command whereof we shall make mention but of 8 of the chief Spirits that belong to the Day & as many that belong to the Night, who hath 20 servants apeice to attend them, when they are called forth to appearance, they are very loving and courteous, willing to do your will, you must call those in the Day that belong to the Day, & those in the Night that belong to the Night, whose names & seals are as followeth.

The Conjuration:

*"I Conjure thee O thou Mighty & Potent Prince Gediel, &c."*

# THE SEALS OF GEDIEL'S 8 CHIEF SPIRITS BELONGING TO THE DAY:

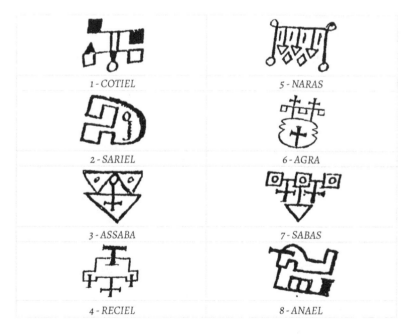

| | |
|---|---|
| 1 - COTIEL | 5 - NARAS |
| 2 - SARIEL | 6 - AGRA |
| 3 - ASSABA | 7 - SABAS |
| 4 - RECIEL | 8 - ANAEL |

# THE SEALS OF GEDIEL'S 8 CHIEF SPIRITS BELONGING TO THE NIGHT:

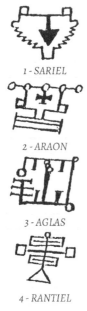

1 - SARIEL

2 - ARAON

3 - AGLAS

4 - RANTIEL

5 - CIRECAS

6 - VRIEL

7 - MISHEL

8 - BARIEL

# 11 - ASYRIEL

Ruling in the Southwest part of the World, & hath 20 great Dukes to attend him in the Day & as many in the Night, who have under them several servants to attend them, & we mention 8 of the chief Dukes that belong to the Day & as many that belong to the Night, because they are sufficient for practise, & the first 4 that belong to the Day hath 40 servants apeice under them & so hath the first 4 that belong to the Night, & the last 4 of the Day, 20 & the last 4 of the Night 10 apeice. They are all good natured & willing to obey thee, those that are of the Day to be called in the Day, & those of the Night, in the Night, & these be their names & seals that followeth.

The Conjuration:

*"I Conjure thee O thou Mighty & Potent Prince Asyriel, who rulest as a King, &c.*

# THE SEALS OF ASYRIEL'S 8 DUKES BELONGING TO THE DAY:

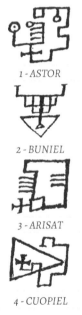

1 - ASTOR

2 - BUNIEL

3 - ARISAT

4 - CUOPIEL

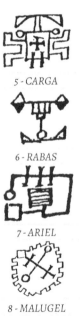

5 - CARGA

6 - RABAS

7 - ARIEL

8 - MALUGEL

# THE SEALS OF ASYRIEL'S 8 DUKES BELONGING TO THE NIGHT:

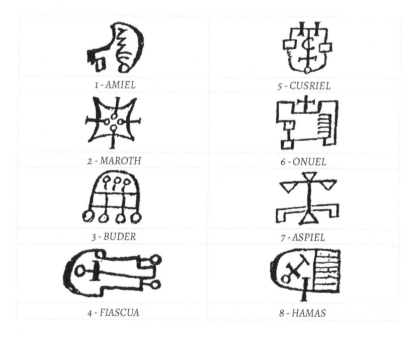

1 - AMIEL

2 - MAROTH

3 - BUDER

4 - FIASCUA

5 - CUSRIEL

6 - ONUEL

7 - ASPIEL

8 - HAMAS

# 12 - MASERIEL

The 8th. Spirit in order but the 4th. under the Empire of the South is called Maseriel, who ruleth as King in the Dominion of the West & by South, & hath a great number of Princes & Servants under him to Attend him, whereof we shall make mention of 12 of the chief spirits that attend him in the day time & 12 that attend & do his will in the night time, which is sufficient for practise, they are all good natured & willing to do your will in all things, those that are for the day are to be called in the day, & those for the night, in the night, their names & seals followeth & each Spirit hath 30 servants to attend him.

The Conjuration:

*"I Conjure thee O thou Mighty & Potent Prince Maseriel, who Ruleth as King, &c"*

# THE SEALS OF MASERIEL'S 12 CHIEF SPIRITS BELONGING TO THE DAY:

| | |
|---|---|
| 1 - MAYHUC | 7 - CHAROS |
| 2 - ZERIEL | 8 - ALIEL |
| 3 - AZIMEL | 9 - EARVIOL |
| 4 - ASSUEL | 10 - VESCUR |
| 5 - ROVIEL | 11 - PATIEL |
| 6 - ATNIEL | 12 - ESPOEL |

# THE SEALS OF MASERIEL'S 12 CHIEF SPIRITS BELONGING TO THE NIGHT:

1 - ARACH

2 - SARMIEL

3 - BARAS

4 - RABIEL

5 - NARAS

6 - AMOYR

7 - ELIEL

8 - ATRIEL

9 - NOGEIEL

10 - BADIEL

11 - EAROS

12 - SOLVAR

# 13 - MALGARAS

The 9th. Spirit in order but the first under the Empire of the West is called Malgaras, he ruleth in the Dominion of the West & hath 30 Dukes under him in the day & as many for the night, & they every one of them have 30 servants to attend them excepting Miliel, Barfas, Asper & Deiles for they have but 20 apeace. Arois & Basiel hath but 10, and they are all very courteous & will appear willing to do your will, they appear 2 & 2 at a time with their servants, those that are for the day to be called in the day, & those of the night in the night, their names &c. as followeth.

The Conjuration:

*"I Conjure thee O thou mighty & potent Prince Malgaras, &c."*

# THE SEALS OF MALGARAS' 12 SERVANTS BELONGING TO THE DAY:

1 - CARIMIEL

2 - AGOR

3 - UDIEL

4 - MELIEL

5 - CASIEL

6 - ORIEL

7 - RABIEL

8 - ALISIEL

9 - BORAS

10 - CABIEL

11 - BARFAS

12 - AROIS

# THE SEALS OF MALGARAS' 12 SERVANTS BELONGING TO THE NIGHT:

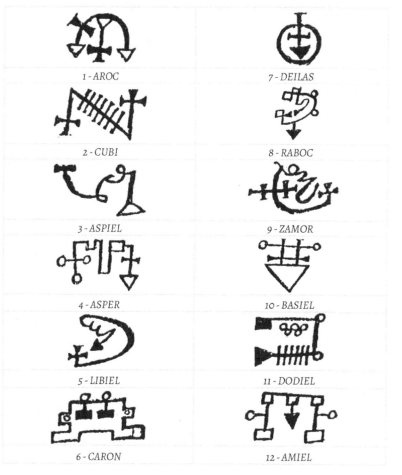

| | |
|---|---|
| 1 - AROC | 7 - DEILAS |
| 2 - CUBI | 8 - RABOC |
| 3 - ASPIEL | 9 - ZAMOR |
| 4 - ASPER | 10 - BASIEL |
| 5 - LIBIEL | 11 - DODIEL |
| 6 - CARON | 12 - AMIEL |

# 14 - DAROCHIEL

The 10th. Spirit in order but the second under the Empire of the West is Dorochiel, who is a mighty Prince ruling in the West & by North & hath 40 Dukes to attend on him in the day & as many for the night, with an inumerable company of servants, whereof we shall make mention of 24 chief Dukes that belong to the day & as many for the night, with their seals as followeth. Note the 12 first that belong to the Day & of the Night hath 40 servants apiece to attend them when they appear, & all these of the day are to be called in the day, & those of the night in the night. Observe the planetary motions in calling, for the two first that belongeth to the day are intended for the first planetary hour, of the 2 next for second planetary hour of the day, & so successively on till you have gone through the day to the night, & through the night till you come to the 2 first of the day again, & they are all of good nature & are willing to obey & do your will, their names & seals are as followeth

The Conjuration:

*"I Conjure thee, O thou mighty & Potent Prince Dorochiel, &c."*

# DAROCHIEL'S 24 DUKES BELONGING TO THE DAY, THE SEALS OF THE 12 DUKES BELONGING BEFORE NOON:

| | |
|---|---|
| 1 - MAGAEL | 7 - FUBIEL |
| 2 - CARCIEL | 8 - ASPHOR |
| 3 - GUDIEL | 9 - DANAEL |
| 4 - ABRIEL | 10 - ARTINO |
| 5 - CHORIEL | 11 - CORBA |
| 6 - EMUEL | 12 - ALSHOR |

150

1 - LOMOR

2 - ETIEL

3 - MERACH

4 - SOVIEL

5 - CASAEL

6 - MAMEL

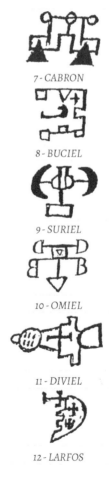

7 - CABRON

8 - BUCIEL

9 - SURIEL

10 - OMIEL

11 - DIVIEL

12 - LARFOS

151

# DAROCHIEL'S 24 DUKES BELONGING TO THE NIGHT, THE SEALS OF THE 12 DUKES BELONGING BEFORE MIDNIGHT:

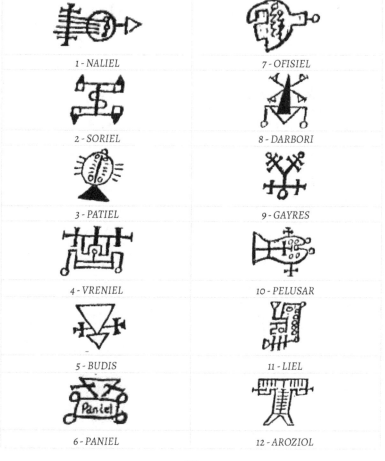

| | |
|---|---|
| 1 - NALIEL | 7 - OFISIEL |
| 2 - SORIEL | 8 - DARBORI |
| 3 - PATIEL | 9 - GAYRES |
| 4 - VRENIEL | 10 - PELUSAR |
| 5 - BUDIS | 11 - LIEL |
| 6 - PANIEL | 12 - AROZIOL |

## DAROCHIEL'S 24 DUKES BELONGING TO THE NIGHT, THE SEALS OF THE 12 DUKES BELONGING AFTER MIDNIGHT:

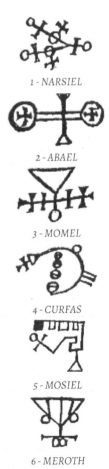

1 - NARSIEL

2 - ABAEL

3 - MOMEL

4 - CURFAS

5 - MOSIEL

6 - MEROTH

7 - CHADRIEL

8 - GARIEL

9 - MAZIEL

10 - CUSIJND

11 - LOBIEL

12 - PASIEL

# 15 - USIEL

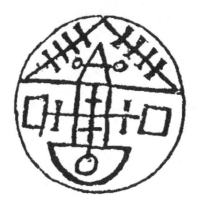

The 11th. Spirit in order but the third under the Emperor Amenadiel, is called Usiel, who is a mighty Prince ruling as King in the Northwest, he hath 40 diurnal & 40 nocturnal Dukes to attend him, in the day & in the night, whereof we shall make mention of 14 that belong to the day & as many for the night, which is sufficient for practise, the first 8 that belong to the day hath 40 servants apiece & the others 630 apiece, & the first 8 that belong to the night hath 40 servants apiece to attend them & the next 4 Dukes have 20 servants, and the last 2 Dukes hath 10 apiece, & they are very obedient & do willingly appear when they are called, they have more power to hide or discover treasure than any other Spirits saith Solomon, that is contained in this book Theurgia Goetia, & when you hide & would not have any thing taken away that is yours, make these 4 seals in virgin parchment & lay them with the treasure or where the treasure lyeth & it will never be found nor taken away, the names & seals of the Spirits are as followeth:

The Conjuration:

*"I Conjure thee O thou mighty & Potent Prince Usiel, &c."*

# USIEL'S 14 DUKES BELONGING TO THE DAY:

1 - ABARIEL

2 - AMETA

3 - AMEN

4 - HERNE

5 - SADFAR

6 - POTIEL

7 - FABARIEL

8 - SEAFAR

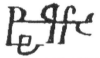

9 - MAPUI

10 - AMANDIEL

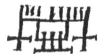

11 - BARFU

12 - GARNAFU

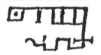

13 - HISIAM

14 - USINIEL

# USIEL'S 14 DUKES BELONGING TO THE NIGHT:

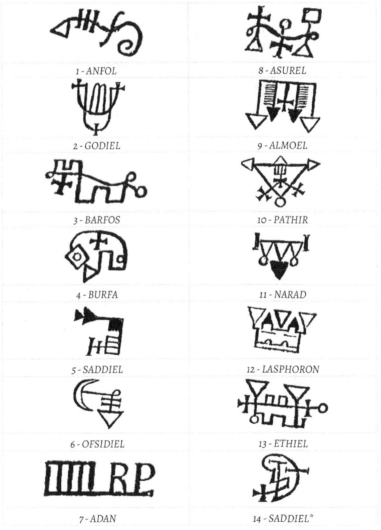

| | |
|---|---|
| 1 - ANFOL | 8 - ASUREL |
| 2 - GODIEL | 9 - ALMOEL |
| 3 - BARFOS | 10 - PATHIR |
| 4 - BURFA | 11 - NARAD |
| 5 - SADDIEL | 12 - LASPHORON |
| 6 - OFSIDIEL | 13 - ETHIEL |
| 7 - ADAN | 14 - SADDIEL* |

*This seal should haue been between Burfa & Saddiel

# 16 - CABARIEL

The 12th. Spirit in order but the 4th. under the Empire of the West is Cabariel, who is a mighty prince ruling in the West & by North, he hath 50 Dukes to attend him in the day & as many for the night; with them are many servants to attend them, whereof we shall make mention but of 10 of the Chief Dukes that belong to the Day & as many for the Night, & every one of them hath 50 servants to give attendance when their master is called, & note that those that belong to the day are very good & willing to obey their master, & are to be called in the day time, & those of the night are by nature evil & disobediant & will deceive you if they can, & they are to be called in the night, their names & seals of them all are as followeth.

The Conjuration:

*"I Conjure thee o thou mighty & potent Prince Cabariel &c: who ruleth as king in the North & by West &C."*

# THE SEALS OF CABARIEL'S 10 DUKES BELONGING TO THE DAY:

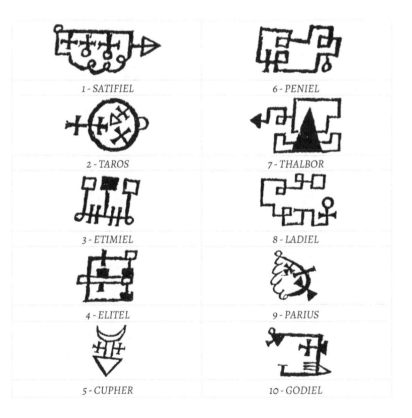

1 - SATIFIEL

6 - PENIEL

2 - TAROS

7 - THALBOR

3 - ETIMIEL

8 - LADIEL

4 - ELITEL

9 - PARIUS

5 - CUPHER

10 - GODIEL

# THE SEALS OF CABARIEL'S 10 DUKES BELONGING TO THE NIGHT:

1 - AFORIEL

2 - ELIJSAM

3 - ANIEL

4 - MADOR

5 - UGIEL

6 - ORIJM

7 - MORIAS

8 - CAZSUL

9 - DUBIEL

10 - PANDOR

# 17 - RAYSIEL

The 13th. Spirit in order, is called Rasiel, he ruleth as King in the North; and hath 50 Dukes for the day, & as many for ye Night to attend him; and they have many servants under them Againe; for as to do their will &c.

Whereof we shall make mention of 16 Chiefe Dukes that belong to the day because they are by nature good & willing to obey; & but 14 that belong to the Night because they are by nature evil & stuborne & disobedient & will not obey willingly.

All these dukes that belong to the day hath 50 servants Apiece excepting the 6 last for they have but 30 apiece; & the 8 first that belong to the Night hath 40 servants Apiece; excepting the 4 next following for they have but 20 apiece; and the last but 10 apiece; Their Names and Seals are as followeth.

The Conjuration:

*"I Conjure thee O Thou mighty & Potent Prince &c."*

## RAYSIEL'S 16 DUKES BELONGING TO THE DAY:

1 - BACIAR

2 - THOAC

3 - SEQUIEL

4 - SADAR

5 - TERATH

6 - ASTAEL

7 - RAMICA

8 - THARAS

9 - DUBARUS

10 - ARMENA

11 - ALBADUR

12 - CHANAEL

13 - FURSIEL

14 - BETASIEL

15 - MELCHA

16 - VUIEL

## RAYSIEL'S 14 DUKES BELONGING TO THE NIGHT:

1 - THARIEL

2 - PARAS

3 - ARAYL

4 - CULMAR

5 - LAZABA

6 - ALEASY

7 - SEBACH

8 - QUIBDA

9 - BELSAY

10 - MORAEL

11 - SARACH

12 - AREPACH

13 - LAMAS

14 - THUREAL

# 18 - SYMIEL

The 14th Spirit in order [but the second under the Empire of the North is called Symiel, who ruleth as King in the North & by East; who hath 10 Dukes to attend him in the day, and a 1000 for the night; & Every one of them hath a Certaine Number of servants whereof we shall make mention of the 10 that belong to the day; and 10 of those that belong to ye night; & those of the day are very good and not disobedient; as those of the night are, for they are stuborn, and will not Appear willingly, &c. Also those Dukes of the day hath 720 servants among them to do their will; & those 10 of the night hath 790 servants to attend on them as occasion serves: The names of these 20 is as followeth; with their seals & numbers of servants, &c.

The Conjuration:

*"I Conjure thee O thou Mighty & Potent Prince; &c."*

| | |
|---|---|
|  |  |
| *1 - ASMIEL 60* | *6 - LARAEL 60* |
|  |  |
| *2 - CHRUBAS 100* | *7 - ACHOT 60* |
|  |  |
| *3 - VAFROS 40* | *8 - BONIEL 90* |
|  |  |
| *4 - MALGRON 20* | *9 - DAGIEL 100* |
|  |  |
| *5 - ROMIEL 80* | *10 - MUSOR 110* |

*1 - MAFRUS 70*

*2 - APIEL 30*

*3 - CURIEL 40*

*4 - MOLAEL 10*

*5 - ARAFOS 50*

*6 - MARIANU 100*

*7 - NARZAEL 210*

*8 - MURAHE 30*

*9 - RICHEL 120*

*10 - NALAEL 130*

# 19 - ARMADIEL

The 15th. Spirit in order [but the 3rd. under the Empire of the North] is called Armadiel, who ruleth as King in the North East Part; and hath many Dukes under him, besides other servants; where of we shall make mention of 15, or the Chiefe Dukes, which hath 1260 servants to attend them; these Dukes are to be called in the day & night, dividing the same into 15 parts; beginning at Sunrise with the first Spirit, & so on till you come to the last Spirit & the last division of the Night; these Spirits are all good by nature; & willing to do your will in all things; these be their Names & seals; &c.

The Conjuration:

*"I Conjure thee O thou Mighty & Potent Prince Armadiel; &c."*

# ARMADIEL'S 15 DUKES:

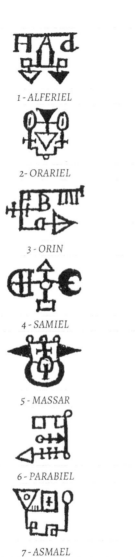

1 - ALFERIEL

2 - ORARIEL

3 - ORIN

4 - SAMIEL

5 - MASSAR

6 - PARABIEL

7 - ASMAEL

8 - IAZIEL

9 - PANDIEL

10 - CARASIBA

11 - LAIEL

12 - CALUARNIA

13 - ASBIBIEL

14 - MAFAYR

15 - OENIEL

167

# 20 - BARUCHAS

The 16th. Spirit in order [but the 4th. under the Empire of the North] is called Baruchas, who ruleth as King in the East & by North; & hath many Dukes and other servants to Attend him; Whereof we shall make mention of 15 of the Chief Dukes; that belong to the day and night, who hath 7040 servants to attend on them; they are all by nature good; and are willing to obey; &c. You are to call these Spirits in the same manner as is showed in the foregoing Experiment of Armadiel; and his Dukes, that is in Dividing the day & night into 15 parts; &c.

The Conjuration:

*"I Conjure thee O thou Mighty & Potent Prince Baruchas; &c."*

## BARUCHAS' 15 DUKES:

1 - QUITA

2 - SARAEL

3 - MELCHON

4 - CAVAYR

5 - ABOC

6 - CARTAEL

7 - IANIEL

8 - PHAROL

9 - BAOXAS

10 - GERIEL

11 - MONAEL

12 - CHUBOR

13 - LAMAEL

14 - DORAEL

15 - DECANIEL

169

## THE WANDERING PRINCES

In this place we are to give you the understanding of all the Mighty and Potent Princes; with their servants, which wandereth up & downe in the Ayre & never Continueth in one place; &c.

170

# 21 - GERADIEL

Whereof of one of the Chiefe & first is Called Geradiel; who hath 18150 servants to attend him; for he hath no Dukes nor Princes; Therefore he is to be invocated Alone; but when he is called, there comes a great number of his servants with him; but more or less according to the hour of the day or night he is called in; for the 2 first hours of the day according to ye Planetary Motion and the 2 second hours of the Night, there comes 470 of his servants with him; And in the 2 second hours of the day; & the 2 third hours of the night there comes 500 of his servants with him; & in the 2 third hours of the day and the 2 fourth hours of the night there comes 930 of his servants with him; and in the 2 fourth hours of the day; & the 2 fifth hours of the night there comes 1560 of his servants; &c and the 2, 5th. hours of the day, and the 2, 6th. hours of the night there comes 13710 of his servants, & in the 2 sixth or last hours of the day there comes 930 servants; & in the first 2 hours of the night there comes 1560 of his servants, &c. They are all indifferent good by nature, and will obey in all things willingly; &c.

The Conjuration:

*"I Conjure thee O thou Mighty and Potent prince Geradiel, who wandereth here and there in the Ayre; with thy servants; I Conjure ye Geradiel that thou, forthwith Appeare with thy Attendants in this first hour of the day here before Me in this Crystal Stone, or here before this Circle, &c.".*

# 22 - BURIEL

The next of these wandering Princes is called Buriel; who hath many Dukes and other Servants, which Doth Attend on him to doe his will, they are all by nature evil; and are hated by all other Spirits; they Appear Rugish; & in the forme of a Serpent with a Virgins head; and Speaketh with a mans voyce, they are to be called in the night, because they hate the day and in the Planetary hours, whereof wee shall mention 12 of the Chiefe Dukes that answereth to the 12 Planetary hours in the night; who hath 880 servants to Attend on them in the night; Their Names and Seals are as followeth; &c.

The Conjuration:

*"I Conjure thee O thou Mighty and Potent prince Buriel, who wandereth here and there in the Ayre; with thy Dukes &other thy servant Spirits; I Conjure thee Buriel that thou forthwith Appear with thy Attendents in this first hour of the night, here before me in this Crystal Stone or here before this Circle in a faire and Comely Shape, to do my will in all things that I shall desire of you; &c."*

# THE SEALS OF BURIEL'S 12 DUKES BELONGING TO THE NIGHT:

1 - MEROSIEL

7 - NEDRIEL

2 - ALMADIEL

8 - FUTIEL

3 - CUPRIEL

9 - DRUSIEL

4 - BUSIEL

10 - CARNIEL

5 - SARVIEL

11 - DRUBIEL

6 - CASBRIEL

12 - NASTROS

# 23 - HIDRIEL

The 3rd. of these wandring Princes is Called Hidriel, who hath 100 Great Dukes besides 200 Lesser Dukes; & servants without number; whereof we shall mention 12 of the Chief Dukes who hath 1320 servants to Attend them; they are to be called in the day, as well as in the night Accordingly to the Planetary Motion; the first beginneth with the first hour of the day or night; and so successively on; till you come to the last; they appear in the forme of a Serpent with a Virgins head & face; yet they are very courteous and willing to obey; they delight most in or about waters; & all Moyst Grounds; &c. Their Names & Seals are as followeth

The Conjuration:


*"I Conjure thee O thou Mighty and Potent Prince Hidriel; &c."*

# THE SEALS OF HIDRIEL'S 12 DUKES BELONGING TO THE DAY:

1 - MORTALIEL

2 - CHAMORIEL

3 - PESARIEL

4 - MUSUZIEL

5 - LAMENIEL

6 - BRACKIEL

7 - SAMIEL

8 - DUSIRIEL

9 - CHAMIEL

10 - ARBIEL

11 - LUSIEL

12 - CHARIEL

# 24 - PIRICHIEL

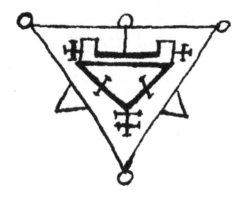

The 4th, in order of these wandring Princes is called Pirichiel; he hath no Princes nor Dukes; but Knights; whereof we shall mention 8 of the Chiefe; These being sufficient for practise; who hath 2000 servants under them; they are to be called According to the Planetary Motion; they are all good by nature and will do your will willingly, their Names and Seals are as followeth.

The Conjuration:

*"I Conjure thee; O thou Mighty & Potent Prince Pirichiel; who wandreth, &c."*

# THE SEALS OF PIRICHIEL'S 8 KNIGHTS:

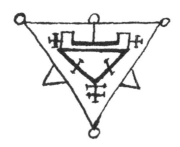

1 - DAMARSIEL

2 - CARDIEL

3 - ALMASOR

4 - NEMARIEL

5 - MENAZIEL

6 - DEMEDIEL

7 - HURSIEL

8 - CUPRISIEL

177

# 25 - EMONIEL

The 5th. Wandring Spirit is called Emoniel, who hath one hundred Princes & Chief Dukes besides 20 under Dukes & a multitude of servants to attend them, whereof we shall mention 12 of the Chief Princes or Dukes who hath 1320 under Dukes & other inferior Spirits to Attend them, they are all by nature good & willing to obey. And they are to be called in the day as well as in the night & according to the Planetary order, it is so they inhabit mostly in woods, their names & seals are as followeth.

The Conjuration:

*"I Conjure thee O thou Mighty & Potent Prince Emoniel, who wanderest, &c."*

1 - ERMONIEL

2 - PANUEL

3 - EDRIEL

4 - CARNODIEL

5 - DRAMIEL

6 - PANDIEL

7 - VASENEL

8 - MASINEL

9 - CRUHIEL

10 - ARMISIEL

11 - CASPANIEL

12 - MUSINIEL

# 26 - ICOSIEL

The 6th. of these Wandring Princes is Called Icosiel, who hath 100 Dukes & 300 Companions besides other servants which are more inferior, whereof we have taken 15 of the Chief Dukes for practise they being sufficient & they have 2000 &c. servants to attend on them, they are all of a good nature & will do what they are commanded, they appear mostly in houses because they delight most there, they are called in the 24 hours of the day & night, that is to divide the 24 hours into 15 parts according to the number of spirits, beginning at the first spirit at Sun Rise & with the last spirit at Sun Setting next day, Their Names & seals are as followeth &c.

The Conjuration:


"I Conjure thee O thou Mighty & Potent Prince Icosiel, &c."

# ICOSIEL'S 15 DUKES:

1 - MACHARIEL

2 - PSICHIEL

3 - THANATIEL

4 - ZOSIEL

5 - ACAPIEL

6 - LERPHIEL

7 - HERACIEL

8 - AMEDIEL

9 - TIANABRIEL

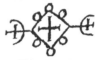

10 - ZACHRIEL

11 - NATHRIEL

12 - ATHESIEL

13 - VRBANIEL

14 - CUMARIEL

15 - MUNETIEL

# 27 - SOTERIEL

The 7th. Spirit of these that wander in the air is called Soteriel, who hath under his command 200 Dukes & 200 Companions who changeth every year their places, they have many to Attend them, they are all good & very obedient, & here we shall mention twelve of the Chief Dukes, whereof the first 6 one year & the other 6 the year following, & so ruleth in order to serve their Prince; who hath under them 1840 servants to attend on them, they are to be called in the day as well as in the night, according to the Planetary Motion, their names & seals are as followeth &c.

The Conjuration:

"*I Conjure thee O thou Mighty and Potent Prince, &c.*"

# THE SEALS OF SOTERIEL'S 12 DUKES:

1 - INACHIEL

2 - PROXEL

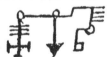

3 - MARUCHA

4 - AMODAR

5 - NADIUSIEL

6 - COBUSIEL

7 - AMRIEL

8 - PRASIEL

9 - AXOSIEL

10 - CAROEL

11 - MURSIEL

12 - PENADER

# 28 - MENADIEL

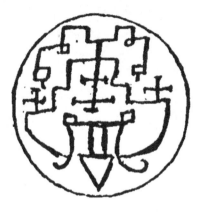

The 8th. of these Wandring Princes is called Menadiel, who hath 20 Dukes & a Hundred Companions & many other Servants, they being all of a good nature & very obedient, here we have mentioned 6 of the Chief Dukes & 6 of the Under Dukes who have 300 servants that attend them & note that you must call these according to the Planetary Motion, a Duke in the first hour & a Companion in the next, & so successively on all the hours of the day & night, whose names & seals followeth, &c.

The Conjuration:

*"I Conjure thee O thou Mighty or Potent Prince Menadiel, &c."*

## THE SEALS OF MENADIEL'S 12 DUKES:

| THE CHIEF DUKES | THE UNDER DUKES |
|---|---|
|  |  |
| 1 - LARMOL | 1 - BARCHIEL |
|  |  |
| 2 - BRASSIEL | 2 - ARMASIEL |
|  |  |
| 3 - CHAMOR | 3 - BARUCH |
|  |  |
| 4 - BENODIEL | 4 - NEDRIEL |
|  |  |
| 5 - CHARSIEL | 5 - CURAIJN |
|  |  |
| 6 - SAMIEL | 6 - THARSON |

# 29 - MACARIEL

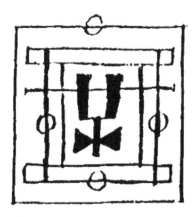

The 9th. Wandring Spirit in order is called Macariel, who hath 40 Dukes besides other inferior servants to attend him, whereof we shall mention 12 of the Chief Dukes which hath 400 servants to Attend them, they are all good by nature and obedient to do the will of the Exorcist, they appear in diverse forms but mostly in the form of a dragon with a virgins head, and these Dukes are to be called in the day as well as in the night, according to the Planetary order, & their names & seals are as followeth, &c.

The Conjuration:


*"I Conjure thee O thou Mighty & Potent Prince Macariel who wandreth, &c."*

# THE SEALS OF MACARIEL'S 12 DUKES:

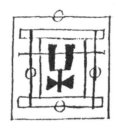

1 - CHANIEL

2 - DRUSIEL

3 - ANDROS

4 - CAROEL

AMADIEL

6 - REMIJEL

7 - NAUSTUEL

8 - VERPIEL

9 - GERMEL

10 - THIRSIEL

11 - BURFIEL

12 - AROMUSIJ

187

# 30 - URIEL

The 10th. Wandring Spirit in order is called Uriel, who hath 10 Dukes & 100 under Dukes with many servants to attend him, they are all by nature Evil & will not obey willingly & are very false in their doings, they appear in the form of a serpent with a virgins Head & face, whereof we shall mention but 10 of the Chief Dukes which hath 650 Companions and servants to attend them, their names & seals are as followeth &c.

The Conjuration:

*"I Conjure thee O thou Mighty & Potent Prince Uriel, &c."*

# THE SEALS OF URIEL'S 10 DUKES:

1 - CHABRI

6 - DRAGON

2 - DARBOS

7 - CURMIS

3 - NARMIEL

8 - DARPIOS

4 - FRASMIEL

9 - HERMON

5 - BRYMIEL

10 - ALDRUSIJ

# 31 - BYDIEL

The 11th & last Spirit & Prince of this Wandring order is called Bydiel, who hath under his command 20 Chief Dukes & 200 other Dukes more inferior besides very many servants, these Dukes changeth every year their office & place, they are all good & willing to obey the Exorcist in all things, they appear very beautiful in human shape, whereof we shall mention 10 of the Chief Dukes who have 2400 servants to attend them, their Names & Seals are as followeth &c.

## THE SEALS OF BYDIEL'S 10 DUKES:

1 - MUDRIEL

2 - CRUCHAM

3 - BRAMSIEL

4 - ARMONIEL

5 - LEMENIEL

6 - CHAROBIEL

7 - ANDRUCHA

8 - MANASAEL

9 - PERSIFIEL

10 - CHREMO

# THE CONJURATION APPROPRIATE
# TO EACH RANK

## THE CONJURATION OF THE WANDERING PRINCES

*"I Conjure thee O thou Mighty & Potent Prince Bydiel, who wanderest here &
there in the Air, with thy Dukes & other of thy servants Spirits, I Conjure thee
Bydiel that thou forthwith appear with thy Attendance in this first hour of the
day here before me in this Crystal Stone [or here before this Circle] in a fair and
comely shape to do my will in all things that I shall desire of you &c"* [Note this
mark: |*| in the Conjuration following & go on from there as it
followeth. That is, in the Conjuration of the Dukes that do not Wander,
below. &c.]

## THE CONJURATION OF THE PRINCES S THAT
## GOVERN THE POINTS OF THE COMPASS

*"I Conjure thee O thou Mighty & Potent Prince Pamersiel, who ruleth as King in
the Dominion of the East under the Great Emperer Carnatiel, I Conjure thee
Pamersiel that you forthwith appear with thy attendents in this first hour of the
day, here before me in this Crystal Stone [or here before this circle] in a fair &
comely shape to do my will in all things that I shall desire of you &c."* [& observe
this (mark) |*| in the Conjuration that follows and go on as followeth.]

## THE CONJURATION OF THE 4 EMPIRES [EMPERORS]

*"I Conjure thee O thou great & Mighty & Potent Prince Carnatiel who is the the
Emperor & Chief King Ruling in the Dominion of the East, I Conjure thee
Carnatiel that thou forthwith appear &c."* [& observe this mark |∧| & go on
from there in the following Conjuration.]

## THE CONJURATION TO THE WANDRING DUKES

*"I Conjure thee O thou Mighty & Potent Duke N, who wanderest here & there with thy Prince N, & other of his & thy servants in the Air, I Conjure thee N that thou forthwith appear &c."* [& note this mark |∧| & go on from there in the following Conjuration.]

## THE CONJURATION OF THOSE DUKES THAT DO NOT WANDER BUT BELONG TO THE PRINCES THAT GOVERN THE POINTS OF THE COMPASS:

*"I Conjure thee O thou Mighty Duke N., Who rulest under the Prince or King N., in the Dominion of the East, I Conjure thee N., that thou appear forthwith |∧| alone or with thy servants, in this first [or second] hour of the day, here before me in this Crystal Stone [or before this Circle] in a fair & comely shape to do my will in all things that I shall desire or request of you. |\*| I conjure & powerfully command you N. by him that said the word & it was done & by all the holy & powerful names of God who is the only Creator of Heaven and Earth and Hell & what is Contained in them, Adonay, El, Elohim, Elohe, Elion, Escerchi, Zebaoth, Jah, Tetragram-maton Sadai, the only Lord God of hosts, that you forthwith appear unto me here in this Crystal Stone [or here before this Circle] in a fair & comely Human shape without hurt to me or any other Creature that the great God Jehovah hath Created & made, and come ye peaceably, visibly and affably without delay Manifesting what I desire, being conjured by the name of the Eternal Living true God Heliorin Tetragrammaton Anepheneton & fulfill my Commands & Persist unto the end, I conjure, Command & Constrain you Spirit N. by Alpha & Omega & by the name Primeumaton which commandeth the Whole Host of heaven & by all these names which Moses named when he by the power of these names brought great plagues upon Pharaoh & all the people of Egypt; Zebaoth, Escerchie, Oriston, Elian, Adonay primeumaton, & by the name Schersieta Mathia which Joshua called upon the Sun stayed its course; & by the Hagioss & by the Seal of Adonay, & by Agla on Tetragrammaton to whom all creatures are obedient & by the dreadful Judgement of the most high God & by the holy Angels of heaven & by the mighty wisdom of the omnipotent God of hosts*

*that you come from all parts of the world & make rational Answers to all things that I shall ask of you & come ye peaceably & visibly & affably speaking to me with a voice intelligible & to my understanding, therefore come ye, come ye, in the name of Adonay Zebaoth, Adonay Aamioram, come, why stay ye, hasten Adonay Saday the King of Kings Commands you."*

When he appears, show him the seal & pentacle of Solomon saying:

*"Behold the Pentacle of Solomon which I have brought before your presence &c."*

as it is showed in the first book Goetia at the latter end of the Conjurations, also when you have had your desire of the Spirit, license him to depart as is showed there in the book Goetia, &c.

*SO ENDETH THE SECOND BOOK CALLED*

*THEURGIA GOETIA.*

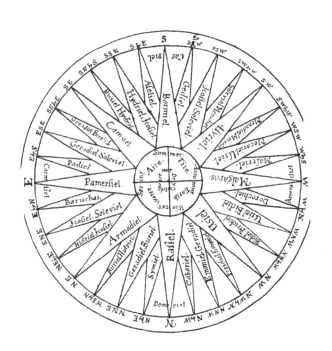

# THE LESSER KEY OF SOLOMON

# LEMEGETON

## BOOK III, ARS PAULINA

SOURCE MATERIAL

*SLOANE MS. 2731*

# HERE BEGINNETH THE THIRD BOOK,
## CALLED THE

# ARS PAULINA

## OF SOLOMON THE KING

& this is divided into two parts, the first the Angels of the Hours of the Day & Night, the second the Angels of the signs of the Zodiack, as hereafter followeth.

The nature of the 24 Angels of the Day & Night changeth every day & their offices is to do all things that is attributed to the 7 Planets but that changeth every day also, as for example, you may see in the following treatise is that the Angel Samael ruleth the first hour of the day beginning at Sun Rising, supposing it to be on a Monday, in the first hour of the day that is attributed to the Moon, and you call Samael or any of his Dukes, their offices in that hour is to do all things that is attributed to the Moon but if you call him or any of his servants Dukes on a Tuesday morning at Sunrising being the first hour of the Day their offices is to do all things that is attributed to Mars & so the like rule is to be observed in the first hour of every day & the like is to be observed of the Angels & their servants that ruleth any of the other hours either in the Day or Night, also again there is an observation [rule] to be observed in making the seals of the 24 Angels, according to the time of the year, day and hour that you call the Angel or his servants in to do your will, but you cannot mistake therein if you do but observe the example that is laid down in the following work, they being all fitted for the tenth day of March, being on a Wednesday in the year 1641 according to the old account. To know what is attributed to the 7 Planets, I do refer you to the books of Astrology whereof large volumes hath been written.

When the seal is made according to the former directions, lay it upon the Table of Practice, upon that part of the Table that it notes with the Character that the Lord of the Ascendant is of, lay your hand on the seal & say the Conjuration that is at the latter end of this third part for it serves of all, only changing the names according to the time you work.

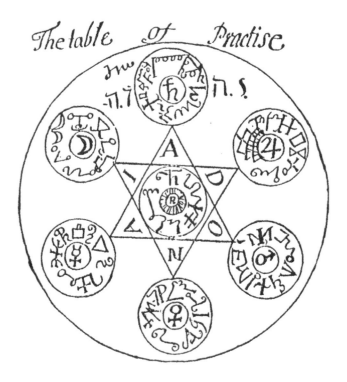

The perfume is to be made of such things as is attributed to the 7 Planets, &c. Note: ♂ is the lord of the Ascendant of every first hour of the day whilst the Sun goes through Aries & Scorpio, so is ♀ the Ascendant every first hour whilst the ☉ goes through ♉ & ♎ so the like of the rest.

# THE 24 HOURS OF THE DAY & NIGHT

## THE 12 HOURS OF THE DAY:

## 1 - SAMAEL

The 1st. hour of the day is ruled by an Angel called Samael, who hath under his command many Dukes & servants whereof we shall mention 8 of the Chief Dukes which is sufficient for practise, who hath 444 servants to attend them, their names are as followeth: Ameniel, Charpon, Darosiel, Monasiel, Brumiel, Nestoriel, Chremas, Meresyn; now to make a seal for any of these 8 Dukes or their Chief Prince Samael, do as followeth, first write the character of the Lord of the Ascendant, secondly the Moon afterwards the rest of the Planets; after that the Characters & Sign that ascends upon the 12th. house in that hour, as it shows in the Sigil following, which is fitted for the 10th. day of March, in the year of our Lord 1641, being on a Wednesday & the first hour of the Day.

# 2 - SEVORMI

The 2nd. hour of the day is called Sevormi, and the Angel that governs this hour is called Anael, who hath 10 chief Dukes to attend him, whereof we shall make mention of 9, but the 3 first are of the Chief & the other 6 are of the under Dukes. They have 330 servants to attend them. These 9 are as followeth: Menerchos, Sarchiel, Cardiel, Orphiel, Elmoijm, Quosiel, Ermoziel, Granijel. & when you have a desire to work in the second hour of Wednesday on the 10th. day of March make a seal before on clean paper or parchment, writing first the character of the Lord of the Ascendant, then the rest of the planets & the Sign of the 12th. house as you see it in the Sigil. & when it is made, lay it on that part of the Table that hath the same Character as the Lord of the Ascendant is. Observe this rule in all the following part you cannot err. Then say the Conjuration at the latter end.

# 3 - DANSOR

The 3rd. hour of the day is called Dansor, & the Angel thereof is called Veguaniel, who hath 20 Chief Dukes & 200 lesser & a great many servants to attend them, whereof we shall mention 4 of the Chief Dukes & 8 of the lesser Dukes who hath 1700 servants to attend them. Their names are as followeth: Ansmiel, Persiel, Mursiel, Zoetiel, Drelmech, Sadimel, Parniel, Comadiel, Gemary, Xautiel, Serviel, Furiel, these being sufficient for practise. Make a seal suitable to the day & hour of the year, as this is for the time before mentioned, & you cannot Err. Then say the Conjuration.

# 4 - ELECHIN

The 4th. hour of the day is called Elechin & the Angel that ruleth that hour is called Vachmiel, who hath 10 Chief Dukes & 100 under Dukes besides many servants, whereof we shall mention 5 of the Chief Dukes & 10 of the under Dukes, who hath 155 servants to attend them. Their names are as followeth: Ammiel, Larmiel, Marfiel, Ormijel, Zardiel, Emerfiel, Permiel, Queriel, Serubiel, Daniel, Jermiel, Thuzez, Vanesiel, Zasviel, Harmiel, they being sufficient for practise. Make a seal suitable for this hour as before directed, & you cannot err. The form of it will be as this is here for the time before mentioned & when it is made, do as you were before directed. Then say the Conjuration.

# 5 - TEALEACH

The 5th. hour of every day is called Tealeach & the Angel ruling it is called Sasquiel, he hath 10 Chief Dukes & 100 lesser Dukes & many servants, whereof we shall mention 5 of the Chief & 10 of the lessor Dukes who hath 5550 servants to attend them. Their names is: Damiel, Aramiel, Maroch, Serapiel, Putrsiel, Jameriel, Futuniel, Ramesiel, Amisiel, Omezach, Lameros, Zathiel, Fustiel, Bariel, being sufficient for practise. Then make a seal suitable for the time, as I have here given you an example of, for the Day aforesaid & year 1641. When you have made it, lay it upon the table as you were before directed & say the Conjuration.

# 6 - GENPHORIM

The 6th. hour of the day is called Genphorim, & the Angel ruling that hour is called Samiel, who hath 10 Chief Dukes & 100 lesser Dukes besides many other inferior servants, whereof we shall mention 5 of the Chief Dukes & 10 of the lesser, who hath 5550 servants to attend them. Their names are these: Arnebiel, Charuch, Medusiel, Nathmiel, Pemiel, Jamiel, Jenotriel, Sameon, Trasiel, Zamion, Nedaber, Permon, Brasiel, Comosiel, Enader, these being sufficient for practise in this hour of the day. Then make a seal suitable to the time of the year, day & hour as I have made one for the time aforesaid, then lay it on the table as you was before directed & you cannot err. Then say the Conjuration.

# 7 - HEMARIM

The 7th. hour of the day is called Hemarim, & the Angel governing the same is called Bargniel, who hath 10 Chief Dukes & 100 under Dukes besides servants which are very many, whereof we shall make mention of 5 of the Chief Dukes & 10 of the lesser who hath 600 servants to attend them in this hour. Their names are these: Abrasiel, Fermos, Nestori, Mamiel, Sagiel, Harmiel, Naustrus, Varmay, Thusmas, Crosiel, Pastiel, Venesiel, Enarim, Dusiel, Kathos, they being sufficient for practise in this hour, & then make a seal as I give you here an example. Then lay it on the table as you were before directed & having all things in readiness, say the Conjuration.

# 8 - JESAMIN

The 8th. hour of the day is called Jesamin, & the Angel that governs the same is called Osmadiel, who hath 10 Chief Dukes & 100 lessor Dukes besides many other servants, whereof we shall make mention of 5 of the Chief Dukes & 10 of the lesser who hath 3100 servants to attend them, they being sufficient for practise. Their names are: Serfiel, Amatim, Chroel, Mesiel, Lantrhes, Demaros, Janosiel, Larfuti, Vemael, Thribiel, Mariel, Remasin, Theoriel, Framion, Ermiel, & then make a seal for the 8th. hour as is showed by this seal which is made for an example. Then lay it on the table & say the Conjuration.

# 9 - CARRON

The 9th. hour of the day is called Carron & the Angel ruling it is called Vadriel, who hath many Dukes both of the greater & lesser order, besides many other servants which are more inferior, whereof 10 of the greater & 100 of the lesser Dukes hath 192980 servants in order to obey & serve them, whereof we shall mention the names of 5 of greater Dukes & 10 of the lesser Dukes, who hath 650 Chief servants to attend on them in this hour, being sufficient for practise. Their names are these: Astroniel, Charnis, Pamorij, Damiel, Madriel, Chromos, Menos, Brasiel, Nesarin, Zoijmiel, Trubas, Zarmiel, Lameson, Zasnoz, Janediel, & when you have a desire to make an experiment in this hour, make a seal as aforesaid, the form of this for an example & when it is made, lay it on the Table as aforesaid and then say the conjuration.

# 10 - LAMATHON

The 10th. hour in any day is called Lamathon & the Angel ruling it is called Oriel, who hath many Dukes & servants divided into orders which contains 5600 Spirits, whereof we shall mention 5 of the Chief Dukes & 10 of the next lesser Dukes, who hath 1100 servants to attend on them, they being sufficient for practise. Their names are these: Armasi, Darbiel, Penaly, Mefriel, Choreb, Lemur, Oymas, Charnij, Zazior, Naveron, Zantros, Busiton, Nameron, Krunoti, Alfrael. And when you have a desire to practise in this hour, make a seal suitable to the time, as this here is made for the 10th. hour on Wednesday the 10 day of March 1641 &c.

# 11 - MANELOHIM

The 11th. hour in any day is called Manelohim & the Angel governing this hour is called Bariel, who hath many Dukes & servants which are divided into 10 parts which contains 5600 Spirits, whereof we shall mention 5 of the Chief Dukes of the first order & 10 lesser Dukes of the second order, who hath 1100 to attend them, they being sufficient for practise. Their names are these: Almarizel, Parlimiel, Chadros, Turmiel, Lamiel, Menafiel, Demasor, Omary, Hehuas, Zemoel, Ahuas, Perman, Comial, Temas, Lanifiel, & then do all things in order as aforesaid &c.

# 12 - NAHALON

The 12th. hour of every day is called Nahalon & the Angel governing this hour is called Beratiel, who hath many Dukes & other servants which is divided into 12 degrees, the which contain to the number of 3700 Spirits in all, whereof we shall make mention of 5 of the greater Dukes & 10 of the next order who hath a 1100 servants to attend them, they being sufficient for practise. Their names are these: Camaron, Altrafrel, Penatiel, Demarec, Famaris, Pamiel, Nerostiel, Emarson, Uvirix, Sameron, Edriel, Chorion, Romiel, Tenostiel, Uamary, & then make the seal & do as Aforesaid &c.

# 1 - OMALHAVIEN

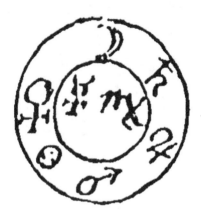

The 1st. hour of every night is called Omalhavien, & the Angel ruling it is called Sabrachon, who hath 1540 Dukes & other servants which are divided into 10 orders or parts, whereof we shall mention 5 of the Chief Dukes & 10 of the next order, they being sufficient for practise. Their names are these: Domaros, Amerany, Penoles, Merdiol, Nastul, Ramasiel, Omedriel, Frandedac, Charsiel, Darnason, Hayzoim, Enalon, Turtiel, Uvenel, Rimaliel. They have 200 servants to attend them. & then prepare your seal suitable to the time & do all things as you were before directed &c.

# 2 - PENAZUR

The second hour of any night is called Penazur & the Angel ruling it is called Taktis, who hath 101550 Spirits to attend him, they being divided into 12 degrees or orders. Whereof we shall mention 6 of the Chief Dukes of the first order & 12 of the next, they being sufficient for practise. Their names are: Almodar, Famoriel, Nedros, Ormezin, Chabril, Praxiel, Parmaz, Vomeroz, Emariel, Fromezin, Ramaziel, Granozy, Gabrynoz, Mezcoph, Tamariel, Venomiel, Janaziel, Zemizim. These have 1320 servants to attend them in this hour, to do their will. & when you will prepare your seal & do it in all things as before directed & you cannot err.

# 3 - GUABRION

The 3rd. hour of every night is called Guabrion, and the Angel governing it is called Sarquamech, who hath 101550 Dukes & servants to attend him, which is divided into 12 degrees or orders, whereof we shall mention 6 Dukes of the first order & 12 of the second order, they being sufficient for practise. Their names are: Menarim, Chrusiel, Penergoz, Amriel, Deminoz, Neztozoz, Evamiel, Sarmezyrs, Haylon, Uvabriel, Thurmytzol, Fromzon, Vanoir, Lemaron, Almonayzod, Janoshyel, Melrotzod, Zanthyozod. These have 1320 servants to attend them. & when you will make any experiment, make a seal proper to the time & do all things as aforesaid &c.

# 4 - RAMERSI

The 4th. hour of the night is called Ramersi, & the Angel governing it is called Jefischa. He hath 101550 Dukes to attend & other servants (which) are divided into orders or degrees to attend him, whereof we shall mention 6 of the Chief Dukes & 12 of those Spirits of the second order, they being sufficient for practise. Their names are: Armosiel, Jvedruan, Maneij, Lozor, Mael, Phersiel, Remezyn, Raisiel, Gemezin, Fresmiel, Haymoyzod, Gapuviel, Jasphiel, Lamodiel, Adroziel, Zodrel, Bromiel, Coreziel, Etnatriel. These have 7260 servants to attend them. & when you have a desire to make an experiment, make your seal & do as aforesaid, &c.

# 5 - SANAYFOR

The 5th. hour of every night is called Sanayfor and its Angel is called Abasdarhon. He has 101550 Dukes & other servants at his command, they being divided 12 degrees or orders, whereof we shall mention 12 of the Dukes belonging to the first order & as many of the second, they being sufficient for practise in this hour. Their names are as followeth: Meniel, Charaby, Appinel, Dematron, Necorin, Hameriel, Vulcamiel, Semelon, Clemary, Venescar, Samerin, Zantropis, Herphatzal, Chrymos, Patrozin, Nameton, Baymasos, Phaytiel, Neszomy, Uvesolor, Carmax, Umariel, Kralim, Habalon, who hath 2400 servants to attend them. Then make your seal according to the time when you go to make an experiment & do all things as aforesaid, & you cannot err.

# 6 - THAASORON

The 6th. hour of the night is called Thaasoron and the Angel governing it is called Zaazenach, who hath 101550 Dukes & other servants to attend him, they being divided into 12 orders, whereof we shall mention 12 of the Chief Dukes in the first order & 6 of the second order, they being sufficient for practise in this hour. Their names are these: Amonzij, Menoyik, Prenostix, Ivamendor, Cherahel, Dramazed, Tuberiel, Humaziel, Lenaziel, Lamerotzod, Xerphiel, Zeziel, Pammon, Dracon, Gemotzol, Gnaviel, Rudozor, Satmon, who hath 2400 servants to attend them, when you go to work, make your seal & do all things as before directed.

# 7 - VENADOR

The 7th. hour of the night is called Venador & its Angel is called Mendrion, who hath 101550 Dukes & other servants to attend him, they being divided into 12 orders, whereof we shall mention 12 of the first Chief Dukes & 6 of the next order, they being sufficient for practise. Their names are: Mumiel, Choriel, Genaritzos, Poudroz, Memesiel, Someriel, Ventariel, Zachariel, Dubraz, Marchiel, Jonadriel, Pomoniel, Rayziel, Tarmitzod, Amapion, Imonyel, Framoch, Machmag, who hath 1860 servants to attend them, when you intend to work, make your seal proper to the time, day & hour, & do all other things as you were before directed.

# 8 - XIMALIM

The 8th. hour of every night is called Ximalim & the Angel ruling is called Narcriel, who hath 101550 Dukes & other servants to attend him, being divided into 12 degrees, whereof we shall mention 12 Dukes on the first order & 6 of the next, they being sufficient for practise in this hour. Their names are: Cambiel, Nedarim, Astrecon, Marifiel, Dramozin, Lustision, Amelzom, Lemozar, Xernisiel, Kanorfiel, Bufanotzod, Jamodroz, Xanoriz, Pastrion, Themax, Hobrazim, Zimeloz, Gramsiel, who hath 30200 servants to attend them. When you intend to work, make your seal to this hour as this example is, and do as aforesaid.

# 9 - ZESCHAR

The 9th. hour is called Zeschar & the Angel ruling is called Pamiel. He hath 101550 Dukes & other servants to attend him (which) are divided into 12 hours, whereof we shall mention 18 of the Chief Dukes. Their names are: Demaor, Nameal, Adyapon, Chermel, Fenadross, Vemasiel, Cmary, Matiel, Xenoroz, Brandiel, Evandiel, Jamriel, Befranzij, Jachoroz, Xanthir, Armapi, Orucas, Saraiel, who hath 1320 servants to attend them. When you intend to work in this hour of the night make a seal proper to the time & do all things else as you were before directed.

# 10 - MALCHO

The 10th. hour of the night is called Malcho & the Angel governing it is called Iasgnarim, which hath 100 chief Dukes & 100 lesser Dukes, besides many other servants whereof we shall mention 6, three of the first & three of the second order, who hath 1628 servants to attend them. Their names are: Laphoriel, Emerziel, Nameroizod, Chameray, Hazariel, Vraniel. Then make a seal & do as you were directed in all things, &c.

# 11 - ALACHO

The 11th. hour of the night is called Alacho, & the Angel governing it is called Dardariel, who hath many Dukes & servants, whereof we shall mention 14 of the Chief Dukes & 7 of the next lesser order, who hath 420 servants to attend them. They are all good & obey Gods laws, their names are: Cardiel, Permon, Armiel, Nastoriel, Casmiros, Damoriel, Fumarel, Masriel, Hariaz, Damer, Alachus, Emeriel, Mavezoz, Alaphar, Hemas, Druchas, Carman, Elamiz, Iatrziul, Lamersy, Hamerytzod. & then make your seal proper to the time & do as aforesaid &c.

# 12 - XPHAN

The 12th. hour of the night is called Xphan & the Angel governing it is called Sarandiel, who hath many Dukes & servants, whereof we shall mention 14 of the Chief & good Dukes & 7 of the next & second order, who hath 420 servants to attend on them. Their names are as followeth: Adomel, Damasiel, Ambriel, Meriel, Denaryzod, Etharion, Kbriel, Marachy, Chabrion, Nestorel, Zachriel, Naveriel, Damery, Namael, Hardiel, Nefrias, Irmanotzod, Gerthiel, Dromiel, Ladrotzod, Melanas. & when you desire to make an experiment, make a seal proper to this hour, observe the day & time of the year, and all other directions as aforesaid &c.

Then say the Conjuration following &c.

# THE CONJURATION

*"O thou Mighty & potent Angel Samael, who rulest the <u>first hour of the day</u>, I the servant of the most high God, do Conjure & instruct thee in the name of the most high omnipotent & immortal God of Hosts Jehovah | \* | Tetragrammaton & by the name & in the name of that God that you owe obediency to, & by the head of your Hierarchy & by the seal of mark you are known in power by, & by the 7 Angels that stands before the Throne of God, & by the 7 Planets & their seals & characters & by the Angel that ruleth the sign of the 12th. house which now ascends in thy first hour, that you would be so graciously pleased to gird up yourself together & by divine permission to move & come from all parts of the world wheresoever you be & show thyself visibly & plainly in this crystal stone to the light of mine eyes, speaking with a voice intelligible & to my understanding, & that you would be favorably pleased that I may have thy familiar friendship & constant society both now and at all times when I shall call thee forth to visible appearance, to inform & direct me in all things that shall seem good & lawful unto the Creator & thee, O thou great & powerful Angel Samael I invocate Adjure Command & most powerfully call you forth from your orders & places of residence to visible appearance in & through these great & mighty incomprehensible Signall & divine name of the great God who wast, is & ever shall be, Adonay Zebaoth, Adonay Amioram, Hagios Aglaon Tetragrammaton & by & in the name Primeumaton which commandeth the whole host of heaven, whose power & virtue is most Effectual for the calling you forth & command you to transmit your rays perfectly to my sight & voice to my ears, in & through this Celestial Stone, that I may plainly see you & perfectly hear you speak unto me, therefore move O thou mighty & blessed Angel Samael, & by his present name of the great God Jehovah, & by the Imperial Dignity thereof, descend & show your self visibly & perfectly in a pleasant & comely form before me in this Crystal Stone to the sight of mine eyes, speaking with a voice intelligible to apprehension, declaring & accomplishing all my desires that I shall ask or require of you, both herein & whatsoever truth or thing also that is just & lawful before the presence of Almighty God the Giver of all good gifts, unto whom I beg that he would be graciously pleased to bestow upon me, O thou servant of mercy Samael, be thou therefore friendly unto me & do for me, as the servant of the most high God, so far as God shall give you power to perform, whereunto I move you both in power & presence to appear, that I may sing with thee his holy Angel O-Napa-ta-man halle-le-la-jah, Amen."*

But before you call any of the Dukes, you are to Invocate the Chief governing Angel that governs the hour of the day or night, as followeth:

*"O thou mighty & potent Angel Samael, who by the decree of the most high King of Glory, Ruler & governor of this first hour of the day, I, the servant of the Highest, do desire & intreat you in & by these 3 great & potent names of God: Agla On Tetragrammaton, & by the power & virtue thereof, to assist & help me in my affaires & by your power & authority to send & cause to come & appear unto me, all or any of those Angels that I shall call by name that are residing under your government, to instruct, help aid and assist in all such matters or things according to their office as I shall desire or request of him or them & that they may do for me as for the servant of the Highest, Amen."*

Then begin as followeth:

*"Thou mighty & potent Angel Ameniel, who is the first & principal Duke ruling by divine pearission under the great & potent Angel Samael, who is the first great & mighty Angel ruling the first hour of the day, I the servant of the most high God do conjure & invocate thee in the name of the most Omnipotent & immortal Lord God of Hosts Jehovah |\*| &c."*

& so on as before, at this mark |\*| in the conjuration of Samael as aforesaid, and when the Spirit is come, bid him welcome, then ask your desire & when you have done, dismiss him according to the order of dismissing.

### & SO ENDETH THE FIRST PART OF THE

# ARS PAULINA

## THE SECOND PART OF THIS BOOK OF SOLOMON OF THE ARS PAULINA, IS AS FOLLOWETH:

This second part contains the Mystical names of the Angels of the Signs in general & also the Angels of every degree of the signs in general, which is called the Angels of men, because that in some one of these signs & degrees every man is born in, therefore he that knows the minutes of his birth, he may know the name of the Angel that governs him, & thereby he may attain to All Arts & Sciences yea, to all the wisdom & knowledge that any mortal man can desire in this world.

But note this, that these Angels that are attributed to the fire hath more knowledge therein than any other, and those of the water hath more knowledge therein than any other, and also those of the earth hath knowledge therein than any other, and likewise those of the air.

And to know which belongs to the fire, earth, air & water, observe the nature of the signs & you cannot err, for those that is attributed Aries is of the same nature Fiery, & so the like in the rest, but if any planet be in that degree that ascends, then that Angel is of the nature of the sign & planet both, & observe the following method & you cannot but obtain your desire &c.

| | | | |
|---|---|---|---|
| ♂ | ♈ | FIRE | AIEL |
| ♀ | ♉ | EARTH | TUAL |
| ☿ | ♊ | AIR | GIEL |
| ☾ | ♋ | WATER | CAEL |
| ☉ | ♌ | FIRE | OL |
| ☿ | ♍ | EARTH | VIOLL |
| ♀ | ♎ | AIR | JAEL |
| ♂ | ♏ | WATER | SOSOL |
| ♃ | ♐ | FIRE | SUIASEH |
| ♄ | ♑ | EARTH | CASUIASAH |
| ♄ | ♒ | AIR | AUSIM |
| ♃ | ♓ | WATER | PASEL |

These be the 12 Angels that are attributed to the 12 signs of the Zodiac, because of those that hath not got the very degree of their nativity, so that they may make use of these Angels, if be so that they know the sign that ascends.

The other Angels which are attributed to every degree of every sign of the Zodiac are as followeth:

# THE ANGELS OF THE DEGREES OF THE ZODIAC

| | ♈ ♂ | ♉ ♀ | ♊ ☿ | ♋ ☾ | ♌ ☉ | ♍ ☿ | ♎ ♀ | ♏ ♂ | ♐ ♃ | ♑ ♄ | ♒ ♄ | ♓ ♃ |
|---|---|---|---|---|---|---|---|---|---|---|---|---|
| *1st* | *Bial* | *Letiel* | *Latiel* | *Sachiel* | *Mechiel* | *Celiel* | *Ibaich* | *Teliel* | *Taliel* | *Chahel* | *Chamiel* | *Lachiel* |
| *2nd* | *Gesiel* | *Niyael* | *Najael* | *Motiel* | *Satiel* | *Lonael* | *Eagiel* | *Joniel* | *Jamael* | *Tomael* | *Tosael* | *Nohiel* |
| *3rd* | *Hacl* | *Sachiel* | *Sachael* | *Stiel* | *Aiel* | *Nosael* | *Lahael* | *Cosiel* | *Casiel* | *Jaajah* | *Jaajeh* | *Sanael* |
| *4th* | *Ganiot* | *Gueliel* | *Gualiel* | *Sachiel* | *Mochiel* | *Sangiel* | *Naviel* | *Laugael* | *Laugael* | *Casmel* | *Camiel* | *Gnasiel* |
| *5th* | *Zaciot* | *Ponoel* | *Pamel* | *Moliel* | *Satiel* | *Knaphel* | *Saziel* | *Naphael* | *Naphadel* | *Lamajah* | *Lashiel* | *Pangael* |
| *6th* | *Cognel* | *Toxisiel* | *Tzisiel* | *Aniel* | *Aniel* | *Patziel* | *Gnachiel* | *Satziel* | *Satziel* | *Naajah* | *Naajah* | *Tzophal* |
| *7th* | *Taphael* | *Kingael* | *Kingael* | *Sasael* | *Masiel* | *Tzakiel* | *Gatiel* | *Gnakiel* | *Gnakiel* | *Sasaial* | *Samael* | *Kphiel* |
| *8th* | *Hael* | *Raphoel* | *Raphiel* | *Magnael* | *Songael* | *Kriel* | *Tzajael* | *Poriel* | *Poriel* | *Gnamiel* | *Gnashiel* | *Ratziel* |
| *9th* | *Caliel* | *Tozael* | *Gnetiel* | *Athiel* | *Aphiel* | *Rathiel* | *Rohiel* | *Tzathel* | *Tzaugel* | *Paajah* | *Paajah* | *Taraziel* |
| *10th* | *Lariot* | *Gonhiel* | *Bahiel* | *Sobael* | *Motziel* | *Tangiel* | *Raliel* | *Kingiel* | *Kabiel* | *Izashiel* | *Tzaniel* | *Mathiel* |
| *11th* | *Nathel* | *Boriel* | *Goriel* | *Makel* | *Sokel* | *Gnabiel* | *Tavael* | *Robiel* | *Rogael* | *Kiniel* | *Kahiel* | *Bongael* |
| *12th* | *Sagnel* | *Gothiel* | *Dathiel* | *Ariel* | *Ariel* | *Bagiel* | *Gnamel* | *Tagiel* | *Tadiel* | *Riajah* | *Raajah* | *Gobiel* |
| *13th* | *Gabiel* | *Dagnel* | *Hogael* | *Sothiel* | *Mothiel* | *Godiel* | *Bangiel* | *Gnadiel* | *Gnahoel* | *Tashiel* | *Tamiel* | *Dagiel* |
| *14th* | *Pegiel* | *Vabiel* | *Vabiel* | *Magnael* | *Sagel* | *Dahiel* | *Gophel* | *Bovael* | *Bovael* | *Gonamiel* | *Gonastiel* | *Hadiel* |
| *15th* | *Gadiel* | *Zegiel* | *Zagiil* | *Abiel* | *Abiel* | *Hovael* | *Datziel* | *Goziel* | *Goziel* | *Baajah* | *Baajah* | *Vahasah* |
| *16th* | *Khoel* | *Chadiel* | *Chadiel* | *Sagel* | *Magiel* | *Vaziel* | *Hokel* | *Dachiel* | *Dachiel* | *Cashiel* | *Gacniel* | *Zavael* |
| *17th* | *Loviel* | *Tohiel* | *Tahoel* | *Madiel* | *Sadiel* | *Zachiel* | *Varziel* | *Hophiel* | *Hophiel* | *Damiel* | *Dashiel* | *Chaziel* |
| *18th* | *Hazael* | *Javiel* | *Javiel* | *Ahiel* | *Ahoel* | *Chotiel* | *Zethel* | *Vajael* | *Vajael* | *Haajah* | *Haajah* | *Tachael* |
| *19th* | *Gociel* | *Chaziel* | *Chazael* | *Lavael* | *Mukel* | *Tijel* | *Chongel* | *Zachiel* | *Zachiel* | *Vashiel* | *Vamiel* | *Jabael* |
| *20th* | *Botiel* | *Bachiel* | *Bachael* | *Maziel* | *Saziel* | *Jochiel* | *Tobielh* | *Chabiel* | *Chabiel* | *Zannel* | *Zashiel* | *Cajoal* |
| *21st* | *Giel* | *Gotiel* | *Gotiel* | *Achiel* | *Achiel* | *Cabiel* | *Jagiel* | *Tagiel* | *Tagiel* | *Chael* | *Chael* | *Bachiel* |
| *22nd* | *Dachael* | *Dajel* | *Dajoel* | *Sotiel* | *Matiel* | *Bagiel* | *Codiel* | *Jadiel* | *Jadiel* | *Tashiel* | *Tamiel* | *Gabael* |
| *23rd* | *Habiel* | *Hachael* | *Hachael* | *Majel* | *Goel* | *Gadiel* | *Bohel* | *Chael* | *Cahael* | *Jmojah* | *Jashiel* | *Dagiel* |
| *24th* | *Vagel* | *Vabiel* | *Vabiel* | *Achael* | *Achael* | *Dahiel* | *Sael* | *Baviel* | *Baviel* | *Ciajah* | *Ciajah* | *Hodiel* |
| *25th* | *Zadiel* | *Zagiel* | *Zagiel* | *Sabiel* | *Mabiel* | *Hovael* | *Daziel* | *Gozael* | *Gozael* | *Boshael* | *Bomiel* | *Vahoiah* |
| *26th* | *Chael* | *Chadiel* | *Chadiel* | *Magiel* | *Sagiel* | *Vasiel* | *Hochiel* | *Dachael* | *Dachael* | *Gamiel* | *Gashiel* | *Zavael* |
| *27th* | *Tavael* | *Tohael* | *Tahiel* | *Adiel* | *Adiel* | *Zachiel* | *Vatiel* | *Hatiel* | *Hatiel* | *Daael* | *Daael* | *Chazael* |
| *28th* | *Jozel* | *Zavael* | *Daiel* | *Sahiel* | *Mahiel* | *Chetivel* | *Zael* | *Vagael* | *Vadael* | *Hoshael* | *Homiel* | *Tachiel* |
| *29th* | *Chiel* | *Chaziel* | *Hoziel* | *Moviel* | *Savael* | *Tazael* | *Chochiel* | *Zachiel* | *Zachiel* | *Vamiel* | *Vashiel* | *Jalael* |
| *30th* | *Heriel* | *Sachael* | *Vachael* | *Aziel* | *Aziel* | *Jachiel* | *Tohiel* | *Casiel* | *Casiel* | *Zaajah* | *Zaajah* | *Cajael* |

These be the Angels of the Signs, & their seals followeth, being 12, every sign one.

# THESE BE THE 12 SEALS WHICH IS ATTRIBUTED TO THE 12 SIGNS AND THE 360 ANGELS AFORESAID

Make this seal of ♂ 1 ounce ☉ 2 Drams ♀ 2 scruples & melt them together when the ☉ enters the first degree ♈ on the day of ♂ . When the ☾ is in the 9 or 10 degree of ♈ make it or finish it.

Make this seal of ♀ 1 ounce ♃ 1 Dram ♂ 1 Scruple ☉ 2 Drams & melt them together in the very point the ☉ enters ♉ & so finish it &c.

Make this seal of ☉ 1 Dram, & ☾ 1 Dram; melt them together when the ☉ enters ♊ & make a lamen thereof when the ☾ is in ♌ or ♓ .

Make this seal of ☾ when the ☉ enters ♋ in the hour of ☾ , she generating & in go

Make this seal when the ☉ enters ♌, of ☉. Then after, when ♃ is in ♓, engrave the first figure, and the other side when the ☾ is in ♓ . It must not come to the fire but once when it is melted.

Make this seal when the ☉ enters ♍, of ♀ 1 Dram ☉ 1 Ounce ☾ 2 Drams ♃ 1 Scruple & melt them on ☉ Day. Then after when ☿ is well aspected on his day, engrave the word & Characters you see in the figure.

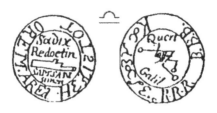

Make this seal of ♀ melted & poured out & made when ☉ enters ♎ .

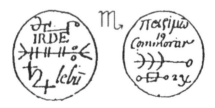

Make this seal when of ♂ on his day & hour when the ☉ enters ♏ & in that hour engrave the fore part of it. Afterward, when the ☉ enters ♈ engrave the other side.

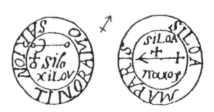

Make this seal when of pure ♃ in the hour of the ☉ enters ♐ & engrave it in the hour of ♃ . This seal is to be hung in a Silver ring.

Make this seal of ☉ & a ring of ♀ to hang it in when the ☉ enters ♑
& engrave it when ♄ is well aspected & in his day and hour.

Make this seal of ☉ 1 Ounce ♄ 2 Drams ♂ 1 Dram & melt them
when the ☉ enters ♒ & engrave it as you see in this figure, when ♄
is in the 9th house.

Make this seal when the ☉ enters ♓ , of ☉ ♂ ♀ & ☽ , of each
2 Drams, of ♃ 1 scruple & let it be melted to engrave the same hour
the ☉ enters ♓ .

.

So when you know the Angel that governs the sign & degree of your Nativity & having the seal ready that belongs to that sign & degree as is showed before, then you are next to understand what order he is of, as is showed herein the following part.

First these genijs that belong to the Fiery Region, that is ♈ ♌ ♐ and governed by Michael the great Angel who is one of the Chief Messengers of God, who is toward the South, therefore these genijs are to be observed in the first hour of a Sunday & at the 8th. hour, also at the 3rd. & 10th. at night, directing yourself toward that quarter, they appear in Royal Apparel holding scepters in their hands, and riding on a Lion or a Cock, their robes are of red & saffron color & most comely, they assume the shape Crowned Queen & very beautiful to behold.

Secondly these genijs that are attributed to ♉ ♍ & ♑ are of the Earthly Regions & are governed by Uriel who hath 3 Princes to attend him: Asaiel, Sochiel & Cassiel. Therefore the genijs that are Attributed to him & these signs are to be observed in the West. They appear like Kings, having green & silver robes, or like little children or women delighting in hunting, & they are to be observed on Saturday in the 1st. & 8th. hours of the day & the 3rd. & 10th. of the night, in those hours you are with privacy to obtain your desires directing yourself towards the west as aforesaid.

Thirdly those genijs that are attributed to ♊ ♎ & ♒ are of the Airy Region whose soverign is called Raphiel, who hath under him 2 princes called Seraphiel & Miel. Therefore these genijs are attributed to him & those signs are to be observed towards the East, on a Wednesday the 1st. hour of the day & 8th., at night the 3rd. & 10th. hours. They appear as Kings or beautiful young men in robes of diverse colors but mostly like women transcendently handsome by reason of their admirable whiteness & beauty.

Fourthly & lastly, these genijs that are attributed to ♋ ♏ & ♓ are of the Watery Regions & are governed by Gabriel who hath under him Samael, Madiel & Mael. Therefore these Genijs that are under these signs & are governed by Gabriel are to be observed on Mondays, towards the North at the 1st. & 8th. hours of the day & at night at the 3rd. & 10th. hours. They appear like Kings having green & silver robes or like little children or women delighting in hunting.

So in the next place, we are to observe the season of the year according to the constellations of the Celestial Bodies, otherwise we shall loose our labor, for if a genijs be of the Igneal Hierarchy its in vain to observe him in any other season but when the ☉ enters these signs which is of his nature, that is ♈ ♌ & ♐ . So if it be a genij of the Earth, he is to be observed when the ☉ enters ♉ ♍ & ♑, & so the like in the rest. Otherwise thus: those genijs that are of the order of Fire are to be observed in the Summer Quarter & those of the Earth in Autumn, those of the Air in Spring, & those of the Water in Winter quarter. Their offices is to do all things that are just & lawful in the sight of the great God Jehovah & what is for our good & what shall concern the protection of our lives or beings or wellbeings & the doing good to our neighbors.

Now he that hath a desire to see his genijs ought to prepare himself accordingly. Now if his genijs be of the Fire, his demands must be for the conservation of his body or person, that he receive no hurt from or by any fire, arms or guns or the like. & having a seal suitable ready prepared he is to wear it when he hath a desire to see his genijs that he may confirm it to him, that for the time to come he may not fail of his assistance & protection upon any occasion. But if his genijs be Aerial, he reconcileth mens natures, increaseth love & affection between them & causeth the desired love of Kings & Princes & secretly promotes Marriages. & therefore he that hath such a genius before he observes him shall prepare a seal suitable to his order, that he may have it confirmed by him in the day & hour of observation, whereof he shall see strange & wonderful effects. & so the like of the other 2 hierarchies.

& when the time is come that you would see your genijs, turn your face to that quarter the sign there is. & that, with prayer to God they being composed to your fancy but suitable to the matter at hand there thou shalt find him & having found him, sincerely acknowledge him, do your duty. Then will he, as being benign & sociable, illuminate your mind, taking away all that is obscure & dark in thy memory & make you knowing in all Sciences sacred & divine in an instant.

Below is a form of prayer which ought to be said upon that coast or quarter where the genijs is several times, it being an Exorcism to call the genij into the Crystal Stone. Note this prayer may be altered to the mind of the worker, for it is here sett for an example.

## THE PRAYER

*"O thou great & blessed N. my Angel Guardian, vouchsafe to descend from thy Holy mansion which is Celestial with thy holy influence & presence into this Crystal Stone, that I may behold thy glory & enjoy thy society, Aid & Assistance both now & forever hereafter, O thou that art higher than the 4th. heaven & knowest the secrets of Elanel, thou that ridest upon the wings of the wind & art mighty & potent in thy Celestial & supersublunary motion, do thou descend & be present I pray thee, I humbly desire & Intreat thee that if ever I have merited thy society or if any of my actions or intentions be real & pure & sanctified before thee, bring thy external presence hither & converse with me, one of thy submissive pupils, in & by the name of the great God Jehovah, whereunto the whole choir of heaven sings continually O Alappa-la-man Hallelujah, Amen."*

When you have said this prayer over several times, as occasion serveth, you will at last see strange lights & passages in the stone & at last you will see your genius, then give him a kind entertainment as you were before directed, declaring unto him your mind & what you would have done.

*SO ENDETH THE THIRD BOOK CALLED*

*ARS PAULINA.*

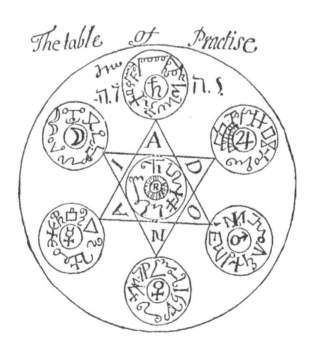

THE LESSER KEY OF SOLOMON

# LEMEGETON

BOOK IV, ARS ALMADEL

SOURCE MATERIAL

*SLOANE MS. 2731*

# HERE BEGINNETH THE FOURTH BOOK
## WHICH IS CALLED THE

# *ARS ALMADEL*

## *OF SOLOMON THE KING*

By this art Solomon attained great wisdom from the Chief Angels that govern the four Altitudes of the World: for you must observe that there are four Altitudes which represent the four Corners of the West, East, North and South: the which is divided into 12 parts; that is, every part 3. And the Angels of every of these parts hath their particular virtues and powers, as shall be showed in the following matter &c.

Make this Almadel of pure white wax; but the others must be coloured suitable to the Altitude. It is to be 4 inches square, and 6 inches over every way, and in every corner a hole, and write betwixt every hole with a new pen those words and names of God following.

But this is to be done in the day and hour of Sol. Write upon the first part towards the East, *ADONAIJ, HELOMI, PINE*. And upon the second towards the South part *HELION, HELOI, HELI*. And upon the West part *JOD, HOD, AGLA*. And upon the Fourth part which is North write *TETRAGRAMMATON, SHADAI, JAH*.

And betwixt the first and the other parts make the pentacle of Solomon thus: ✰ , and betwixt the first quarter write this word *ANABONA*, and in the middle of the Almadel make a Sexangle figure ✧ , and in the middle of it a triangle, wherein must be written these names of God *HELL, HELION, ADONAIJ*, and this last have round about the six-angled figure, as here it is made for an example.

And of the same wax there must be made four candles. And they must be of the same colour as the Almadel is of. Divide your wax into three parts: one to make the Almadel of, and the other two parts to make the candles of. And let there come forth from every one of them a foot made of the same wax to support the Almadel. This being done, in the next place you are to make a seal of pure gold or silver, but gold is best, whereon must be engraved those three names *HELION, HELLUION, ADONAIJ*.

And note that the First Altitude is called Chora Orientis, or the East Altitude. And to make an experiment in this Chora it is to be done in the day and hour of the Sun. And the power and office of those angels is to make all things fruitful, and increase both animals and vegetables in creation and generation, advancing the birth of children, and making barren women fruitful.

And their names are these: *ALIMIEL, GABRIEL, BORACHIEL, LEBES, HELISON*. And note you must not pray for any angel but those that belong to the Altitude you have a desire to call forth.

And when you operate set the four candles upon four candlesticks, but be careful you do not light them before you begin to operate.

Then lay the Almadel between the four candles upon a waxen foot that comes from the candles, and lay the golden seal upon the Almadel, and having the invocation ready written upon virgin parchment, light the candles and read the invocation.

And when he appeareth he appeareth in the form of an Angel carrying in his hand a banner or flag having the picture of a white cross upon it, his body being wrapped round with a fair cloud, and his face very fair and bright, and a crown of rose flowers upon his head.

He ascends first upon the superscription on the Almadel, as it were a mist or fog.

Then must the exorcist have ready a vessel of earth of the same colour as the Almadel is of, and the other of his furniture, it being in the form of a basin, and put thereinto a few hot ashes or coals, but not too much lest it should melt the wax of the Almadel. And put therein three little grains of mastick in powder so that it may fume and the smell go upwards through the holes of the Almadel when it is under it.

And as soon as the Angel smelleth it he beginneth to speak with a low voice, asking what your desire is, and what you have called the princes and governors of this Altitude for.

Then you must answer him, saying:

*"I desire that all my requests may be granted and what I pray for may be accomplished: for your office maketh it appear and declareth that such is to be fulfilled by you, if it please God"*

adding further the particulars of your request, praying with humility for what is lawful and just: and that thou shall obtain from him.

But if he do not appear presently, then you must obtain the golden seal, and make with it three or four marks upon the candles, by which means the Angel will presently appear as aforesaid. And when the Angel departeth he will fill the whole place with a sweet and pleasant smell, which will be smelled for a long time.

And note the golden seal will serve and is used in all the operations of all four Altitudes.

The colour of the Altitude belonging to the first Altitude, or Chora, is lily white; the second Chora a perfect red rose colour; the third Chora is to be a green mixed with a white silver colour; the fourth Chora is to be black mixt with a little green or a sad colour.

## OF THE SECOND CHORA OR ALTITUDE

Note that the other three Altitudes, with their Signs and Princes can exert power over goods and riches, and can make any man rich or poor. And as the first Chora gives increase and maketh fruitful, so these give decrease and barrenness. And if any have a desire to operate in any of these three following Choras or Altitudes, they must do it in die Solis in the manner above showed.

But do not pray for anything that is against God and His laws, but what God giveth according to the custom or course of nature: that you may desire and obtain. All the furniture to be used is to be of the same colour the Almadel is of.

And the princes of the second Chora are named: APHIRIZA, GENON, GERON, ARMON, GEREIMON. And when you operate kneel before the Almadel, with clothes of the same colour, in a closet hung with the same colours also; for the holy apparition will be of the same colours.

And when he appeareth, put an earthen vessel under the Almadel, with fire or hot ashes and three grains of mastick to perfume as aforesaid.

And when the Angel smelleth it he turneth his face towards you, asking the exorcist with a low voice why he hath called the princes of this Chora or Altitude.

Then you must answer as before:

*"I desire that my requests may be granted, and the contents thereof may be accomplished: for your office maketh it appear and declareth that such is to be done by you, if it please God."*

And you must not be fearful, but speak humbly, saying:

*"I recommend myself wholly to your office, and I pray unto you, Prince of this Altitude, that I may enjoy and obtain all things according to my wishes and desires."*

And you may further express your mind in all particulars in your prayer, and do the like in the two other Choras following.

The Angel of the second Altitude appeareth in the form of a young child with clothes of a satin, and of a red rose colour, having a crown of red gilly flowers upon his head. His face looketh upwards to heaven and is of a red colour, and is compassed round about with a bright splendour as the beams of the sun.

Before he departeth he speaketh unto the exorcist saying:

*"I am your friend and brother."*

And illuminateth the air round about with his splendour, and leaveth a pleasant smell which will last a long time upon their heads.

## OF THE THIRD CHORA OR ALTITUDE

In this chora you must do in all things as you were before directed in the other two.

The angels in this Altitude are named: *ELIPHANIASAI, GELOMIROS, GEDOBONAI, SARANAVA & ELOMINA.*

They appear in the form of little children or little women dressed in green and silver colours very delightful to behold, and a crown of baye leaf with white and colours upon their heads. And they seem to look a little downwards with their faces. And they speak as the others do to the exorcist, and leave a mighty sweet perfume behind them.

## OF THE FOURTH CHORA OR ALTITUDE

In this Chora you must do as before in the others, and the Angels in this Chora are called BARCHIEL, GEDIEL, GABIEL, DELIEL & CAPITIEL.

They appear in the form of little men or boys, with clothes of a black colour mixed with a dark green; and in their hands they hold a bird which is naked; and their heads compassed round about with a bright shining of divers colours. They leave a sweet smell behind them, but differ from the others something.

# THE TIMES FOR INVOKING THE ANGELS

Note there is twelve Princes, beside those in the four Altitudes: and they distribute their offices amongst themselves, every one ruling thirty days every year.

Now it will be in vain to call any of the Angels unless it be those that govern then, for every Chora or altitude hath its limited time, according to the twelve signs of the Zodiack; and in that Sign the Sun is in, that or those Angels that belong to that Sign hath the government and should be invoked.

As, for example: suppose that I would call the 2 first of the 5 that belong to the first Chora. Then choose the first Sunday in March, after the Sun hath entered Aries: and then I make an experiment. And so do the like, if you will, the next Sunday after again.

And if you will call the two second that belong to the first Chora, that Sunday after the Sun enters Taurus in April. But if you will call the last of the 5, then you must take those Sundays that are in May after the Sun has entered Gemini, to make your experiment in.

Do the like in the other Altitudes, for they have all one way of working. But the Altitudes have names formed severally in the substance of the heavens, even a Character. For when the Angels hear the names of God that is attributed to them, they hear it by virtue of that Character. Therefore it is in vain to call any angel or spirit unless he knows what name to call him by.

Therefore observe the form of this conjuration or invocation following:

# THE INVOCATION

"O thou great, blessed and glorious Angel of God [N.], who rulest and is the chief governing Angel in the [Number] Chora or Altitude. I am the servant of the Highest, the same your God ADONAIJ, HELOMI, AND PINE, whom you do obey, and is your distributor and disposer of all things both in heaven earth and hell, do invocate, conjure and entreat you [N.] that thou forthwith appear in the virtue and power of the same God, ADONAIJ, HELOMI AND PINE; and I do command thee by him whom ye do obey, and is set over you as King in the divine power of God, that you forthwith descend from thy orders or place of abode to come unto me, and show thyself visibly here before me in this crystal stone, in thy own proper shape and glory, speaking with a voice intelligible to my understanding.

O thou mighty and powerful Angel [N.], who art by the power of God ordained to govern all animals, vegetables and minerals, and to cause them and all creatures of God to spring increase and bring forth according to their kinds and natures: I, the servant of the Most High God whom you obey, do entreat and humbly beseech thee to come from your celestial mansion, and shew unto me all things I shall desire of you, so far as in office you may or can or is capable to perform, if God permit to the same.

O thou servant of mercy [N.], I do humbly entreat and beseech thee by these holy and blessed names of your God ADONAIJ, HELLOMI, PINE; And I do also constrain you in and by this powerful name ANABONA, that you forthwith appear visibly and plainly in your own proper shape and glory in and through this crystal stone, that I may visibly see you, and audibly hear you speak unto me, and that I may have thy blessed and glorious angelic assistance, familiar friendship and constant society, community and instruction, both now and at all times, to inform and rightly instruct me in my ignorance and depraved intellect, judgement and understanding, and to assist me both herein and in all other truths also, through the Almighty ADONAIJ, King of Kings, the giver of all good gifts that his bountiful and fatherly mercy be graciously pleased to bestow upon me.

*Therefore, O thou blessed Angel [N.], be friendly unto me, so far as God shall give you power and presence, to appear, that I may sing with his holy Angels. O Mappa Laman, Hallelujah. Amen.* "

When he appears, give him or them kind entertainment; and then ask what is just and lawful, and that which is proper and suitable to his office.

And you shall obtain it.

*SO ENDETH THE FOURTH BOOK CALLED*

*ARS ALMADEL.*

# THE LESSER KEY OF SOLOMON

# LEMEGETON

## BOOK V, ARS NOTORIA

SOURCE MATERIAL

*"ARS NOTORIA: THE NOTARY ART OF SOLOMON"*

*ROBERT TURNER, 1656*

*THE*

# *NOTORY ART*

*OF SOLOMON THE KING*

# *Ars Notoria* :

## THE

# NOTORY ART

## OF

# *SOLOMON,*

### Shewing the

## CABALISTICAL KEY

Of ⎨ Magical Operations,
The liberal Sciences,
Divine Revelation, and
The Art of Memory.

Whereunto is added

## An Astrological Catechism,

fully demonstrating the Art of
## JUDICIAL ASTROLOGY.

Together with a rare Natural secret, necessary
to be learn'd by all persons; especially
Sea-men, Merchants, and Travellers.

An excellent Invention, done by the Magne-
tick Vertue of the Load-stone.

Written originally in Latine, and now En-
glished by ROBERT TURNER Φιλομαθής.

London, Printed by *J. Cottrel,* and are to be sold
by *Martha Harison,* at the Lamb at the
East-end of Pauls, 1657.

## THE NOTORY ART REVEALED BY THE MOST HIGH CREATOR TO SOLOMON

In the Name of the Holy and undivided Trinity, beginneth this most Holy Art of Knowledge, revealed to Solomon, which the Most High Creator by his Holy Angels ministered to Solomon upon the Alter of the Temple; that thereby in short time he knew all Arts and Sciences, both Liberal and Mechanick, with all the Faculties and Properties thereof: He has suddenly infused into him, and also was filled with all wisdom, to utter the Sacred Mysteries of most Holy words.

*Alpha and Omega!* Oh Almighty God, the Beginning of all things, without Beginning, and without End: Graciously this day hear my Prayers; neither do thou render unto me according to my sins, nor after mine iniquities, O Lord my God, but according to thy mercy, which is greater then all things visible and invisible. Have mercy upon me, O Christ, the Wisdom of the Father, The Light of the Angels, The Glory of the Saints, The Hope, Refuge, and Support of Sinners, The Creator of all things, and Redeemer of all humane Frailties, who holdest the Heaven, Earth, and Sea, and all the whole World, in the palm of thy Hand: I humbly implore and beseech, that thou wilt mercifully with the Father, illustrate my Minde with the beams of thy holy Spirit, that I may be able to come and attain to the perfeion of this most holy Art; and that I may be able to gain the knowledge of every Science, Art, and Wisdom; and of every Faculty of Memory, Intelligences, Understanding, and Intelle×, by the Vertue and Power of thy most holy Spirit, and in thy Name. And thou, O God my God, who in the Beginning hast created the Heaven and the Earth, and all things out of nothing; who reformest, and makest all things by thy own Spirit; compleat, fulfil, restore, and implant a sound understanding in me, that I may glorify thee and all thy Works, in all my Thoughts, Words, and Deeds. O God the Father, confirm and grant this my Prayer, and increase my Understanding and Memory, and strengthen the same, to know and receive the Science, Memory, Eloquence, and Perseverance in all manner of Learning, who livest and reignest, World without end. *Amen.*

*Here beginneth the first Treatise of this Art, which Master Apollonius calleth, The Golden Flowers, being the generall Introduction to all the Natural Sciences; and this is Confirmed, Composed, and Approved by the Authority of Solomon, Manichaeus, and Euduchaeus.*

I, *Apollonius*, Master of Arts, duly called, to whom the Nature of Liberal Arts hath been granted, am intended to treat of the Knowledge of Liberal Arts, and of the Knowledge of Astronomy; and with what Experiments and Documents, a Compendious and Competent Knowledge of Arts may be attained unto; and how the highest and lowest Mysteries of Nature may be competently divided, and fitted and applied to the Natures of Times; and what proper dayes and hours are to be elected for the Deeds and Actions of men, to be begun and ended; what Qualifications a man ought to have, to attain the Efficacy of this Art; and how he ought to dispose of the actions of his life, and to behold and study the Course of the Moon. In the first place there fore, we shall declare certain Precepts of the Spiritual Sciences; that all things which we intend to speak of, may be attained to in order. Wonder not therefore, at what you shall hear and see in this subsequent Treatise, and that you shall find an Example of such inestimable Learning.

Some things which follow, which we will deliver to thee as Essayes of wonderful Effects, and have extracted them out of the most Ancient Books of the Hebrews; which, where thou seest them, (although they are forgotten, and worn out of any humane Language) nevertheless esteem them as Miracles: For I do truly admire the great Power and Efficacy of Words in the Works of Nature.

## OF WHAT EFFICACY WORDS ARE

There is so great Virtue, Power and Efficacy in certain Names and Words of God, that when you read those very Words, it shall immediately increase and help your Eloquence, so that you shall be made Eloquent of Speech by them, and at length attain to the Effects of the powerful Sacred Names of God; but from whence the power hereof doth proceed, shall be fully demonstrated to you in the following Chapters of Prayers: And those which follow next to our hand, we shall lay it open.

## AN EXPLANATION OF THE NOTARY ART

This Art is divided into two parts: the first containeth general Rules, the second special Rules.

We come first to the special Rules, that is, First, to a threefold, and then to a fourfold Division: And in the third place we come to speak of Theologie; which Sciences thou shalt attain to, by the Operations of these Orations, if thou pronounce them as it is written: therefore there are certain Notes of the Notary Art, which are manifest to us; the Virtue whereof Humane Reason cannot apprehend.

The first Note hath his signification taken from the Hebrew; which though the expression thereof be comprehended in a very few words; nevertheless, in the expression of the Mystery, they do not lose their Vertue: That may be called their Vertue, which doth happen and proceed from their pronunciation, which ought to be greatly admired at.

*Hely, Scemath Amazaz, Hemel, Sathusteon, hheli Tamazam, &cet.* which *Solomon* entitled, *His First Revelation*; and that to be without any Interpretation: It being a Science of so Transcendent a purity, that it hath its Original out of the depth and profundity of the *Chaldee, Hebrew,* and *Grecian* Languages; and therefore cannot possible by any means be explicated fully in the poor Thread-bare Scheme of our Language.

And of what nature the Efficacy of the aforesaid words are, Solomon himself doth describe in his Eleventh Book, Helisoe, of the Mighty Glory of the Creator: But the Friend and Successor of Solomon, that is, Apollonius, with some few others, to whom that Science hath been manifested, have explained the same, and defined it to be most Holy, Divine, Deep, and Profound Mysteries; and not to be disclosed nor pronounced, without great Faith and reverence.

## A SPIRITUAL MANDATE OF THE PRECEDENT ORATION

Before any one is to reade or pronounce any Orations of this Art, to bring them to Effect, let them always first reverently and devoutly rehearse the Prayer in the beginning.

If any one will search the Scriptures, or would understand, or eloquently pronounce any part of Scripture, let him pronounce the words of the following Figure, to wit, Hely Scemath, in the morning betimes of that day, wherein thou wilt begin any work.

And in the Name of the Lord our God, let him diligently pronounce the Scripture proposed, with this Prayer which follows, which is, Theos Megale; And is mystically distorted, and miraculously and properly framed out of the Hebrew, Greek, and Chaldee Tongues, and it extendeth itself briefly into every Language, in what beginning soever they are declared.

The second part of the Oration of the second Chapter, is taken out of the Hebrew, Greek, and Chaldee; and the following Expostion thereof ought to be pronounced first, which is a Latine Oration: The third Oration of the three Chapters, always in the beginning of every faculty, is first to be rehearsed.

## THE ORATION IS,
## THEOS MEGTHE, IN TU YMA EUREL, &cet.

This sheweth, how the foregoing Prayer is expounded: But although this is a particular and brief Expostion of this Oration; yet do not think, that all words are thus expounded.

## THE EXPOSITION OF THIS ORATION

*Oh God, the Light of the World, Father of Immense Eternity, Giver of all Wisdom and Knowledge, and of all Spiritual Grace: most Holy and Inestimable Dispenser, knowing all things before they are made; who makest Light and Darkness: Stretch forth thy Hand, and touch my Mouth, and make my tongue as a sharp sword, to shew forth these words with eloquence; Make my Tongue as an Arrow elected to declare thy Wonders, and to pronounce them memorably: Send forth thy holy Spirit, O Lord, into my Heart and Soul, to understand and retain them, and to meditate on them in my Conscience: By the Oath of thy Heart, that is, By the Right-hand of thy holy Knowledge, and mercifully inspire thy Grace into me; Teach and instruct me; Establish the coming in and going out of my Senses, and let thy Precepts teach and correct me until the end; and let the Counsel of the most High assist me, through thy infinite Wisdom and Mercy. Amen.*

## THE WORDS OF THESE ORATIONS CANNOT
## WHOLLY BE EXPOUNDED

Neither think, that all words of the preceding Oration can be translated into the Latine Tongue: for some words of that Oration contain in themselves a greater Sense of Mystical Profundity, of the Authority of Solomon; and having reference to his Writings, we acknowledge; That these Orations cannot be expounded nor understood, by humane sense: For it is necessary, That all Orations, and distinct particulars of Astronomy, Astrology, and the Notory Art, be spoken and pronounced in their due time and season; and the Operations of them to be made according to the disposition of the Times.

## OF THE TRIUMPHAL FIGURES, HOW SPARINGLY THEY ARE TO BE PRONOUNCED, AND HONESTLY AND DEVOUTLY SPOKEN

There are also certain Figures or Orations which Solomon in Chaldeack called, Hely; that is, Triumphal Orations of the Liberal Arts, and sudden excellent Efficacies of Vertues; and they are the Introduction to the Notory Art. Wherefore Solomon made a special beginning of them, that they are to be pronounced at certain determinate times of the Moon; and not to be undertaken, without consideration of the end. Which also Magister Apollonius hath fully and perfectly taught, saying, Whosoever will pronounce these words, let him do it in a determinate appointed time, and set aside all other occasions, and he shall profit in all Sciences in one Moneth, and attain to them in an extraordinary wonderful manner.

## THE EXPOSITIONS OF THE LUNATIONS OF THE NOTARY ART

These are the Expositions of the Lunation, and the Introduction of the Notory Art, to wit, in the fourth and the eighth day of the Moon; and in the twelfth, sixteenth, four and twentieth, eight and twentieth, and thirteenth they ought to be put in operation. From whence Solomon saith, That to those times, we give the expositive times of the Moon; of the fourth day of the Moon, which are written by the four Angels; and in the fourth day of the Moon is manifested to us; and are four times repeated and explained by the Angel, the Messenger of these Orations; and are also revealed and delivered to us that require them from the Angel, four times of the year, to shew the Eloquence and Fulness of the four Languages, Greek, Hebrew, Chaldee and Latine; and God hath determined the Power of the Faculties of Humane Understanding, to the four Parts of the Earth; and also the four Vertues of Humanities, Understanding, Memory, Eloquence, and the Faculty of Ruling those three. And these things are to be used as we have before spoken.

## HE SHEWETH HOW THE PRECEDENT ORATION IS THE BEGINNING AND FOUNDATION OF THE WHOLE ART

That is the first Figure of the Notory Art, which is manifestly sited upon a Quadrangle Note: And this is Angelical Wisdom, understood of few in Astronomy; but in the Glass of Astrology, it is called, The Ring of Philosophy; and in the Notory Art it is written, To be the Foundation of the whole Science. But it is to be rehearsed four times a day, beginning in the morning once, about the third hour once, once in the ninth hour, and once in the evening.

The precedent Oration ought to be spoken secretly; and let him that speaks it be alone, and pronounce it with a low voyce, so that he scarcely hear himself. And this is the condition hereof, that if necessity urge one to do any great works, he shall say it twice in the morning, and about the ninth hour twice; and let him fast the first day wherein he rehearseth it, and let him chastly and devoutly. And this is the Oration which he shall say:

This is the Oration of the four Tongues, Chaldee, Greek, Hebrew and Latine, evidently expounded, which is called, The Splendor or *Speculum* of Wisdom. In all holy Lunations, these Orations ought to be read, once in the morning, once about the third hour, and once in the evening.

### THE ORATION

*Assaylemath, Assay, Lemath, Azzabue.*

The second part of the precedent Orations, which is to be said only once.

*Azzaylemath, Lemath, Azacgessenio.*

The third part of the precedent Oration, which is to be spoken together with the other.

*Lemath, Sabanche, Ellithy, Aygezo.*

## THIS ORATION HATH NO EXPOSITION IN THE LATINE

This is a holy Prayer, without danger of any sin, which Solomon saith, is inexplicable by humane sense.

And he addeth, and saith, That the Explication thereof is more prolixious, than can be considered of or apprehended by Man; excepting also those secrets, which is not lawful, neither is it given to Man to utter: Therefore he leaveth this Oration without Exposition, because no Man could attain to the perfection thereof: and it was left so spiritual, because the Angel that declared it to Solomon, laid an inexcusable prohibition upon it, saying, See that thou do not presume to give to any other, not to expound anything out of this Oration, neither thy self, nor anyone by thee, nor anyone after thee: For it is a holy and Sacramental Mystery, that by expressing the words thereof, God heareth thy Prayer, and increaseth thy Memory, Understanding, Eloquence, and establisheth them all in thee.

Let it be read in appointed times of the Lunation; as, in the fourth day of the Moon, the eighth and twelfth, as it is written and commanded: say that Oration very diligently four times in those dayes; verily believing, That thereby thy study shall suddenly be increased, and made clear, without any ambiguity, beyond the apprehension of humane Reason.

## OF THE EFFICACY OF THAT ORATION WHICH IS INEXPLICABLE TO HUMAN SENSE

This is that onely which Solomon calls The happiness of Wit: and M. Apollonius termeth it, The Light of the Soul, and the Speculum of Wisdom: And, I suppose, the said Oration may be called, The Image of Eternal Life; the Vertue and Efficacy whereof is so great, that is understood or apprehended of by very few or none.

Therefore having essayed some Petitions, Signs and Precepts, we give them as an entrance to those things thereof we intended to speak; of which they are part, that we have spoken of before.

Nevertheless, before we come to speak of them, some things are necessary to be declared, whereby we may more clearly and plainly set forth our intended History: For, as we have said before, there are certain Exceptions of the Notory Art; some whereof are dark and obscure, and others plain and manifest.

For the Notory Art hath a Book in Astronomy, whereof it is the Beginning and Mistriss; and the Vertue thereof is such, that all Arts are taught and derived from her.

And we are further to know, that the Notory Art doth in a wonderful manner contain and comprehend within it self, all Arts, and the Knowledge of all Learning, as Solomon witnesseth: Therefore it is called, The Notary Art, because in certain brief Notes, it teacheth and comprehendeth the Knowledge of all Arts: for so Solomon also saith in his Treatise Lemegeton, that is, in his Treatise of Spiritual and Secret Experiments.

HERE HE SHEWETH, IN WHAT MANNER THESE NOTES DIFFER IN ART, AND THE REASON THEREOF; FOR A NOTE IS A CERTAIN KNOWLEDGE, BY THE ORATION AND FIGURE BEFORE SET DOWN

But of the Orations and Figures, mention shall be made in their due place, and how the Notes are called in the Notory Art.

Now he maketh mention of that Oration, which is called, The Queen of Tongues: for amongst these Orations, there is more excellent than the rest, which King Solomon would therefore have be called, The Queen of Tongues because it takes away, as it were, with a certain Secret covering the Impediments of the Tongue, and giveth it a marvellous Faculty of Eloquence.

Wherefore before we proceed further, take a little Essay of that Oration: For this is an Oration which in the Scriptures we are taught to have alwayes in our mouthes; but it is taken out of the Chaldean Language: which, although it be short, is of a wonderful Vertue; that when you reade that Scripture, with the Oration before-mentioned, you cannot keep silent those things, which the Tongue and Understand suggest, and administer to thee.

The Oration which follows, is a certain Invocation of the Angels of God, and it provoketh Eloquence, and ought to be said in the beginning of the Scripture, and in the beginning of the Moneth.

## THE ORATION

*Lameth, Leynach, Semach, Belmay, Azzailement, Gesegon, Lothamasim, Ozetogomaglial, Zeziphier, Josanum, Solatac, Bozefama, Defarciamar, Zemait, Lemaio, Pheralon, Anuc, Philosophi, Gregoon, Letos, Anum, Anum, Anum.*

## HOW THE ORATION IS TO BE SAID IN THE BEGINNING OF EVERY MONETH, CHASTLY, AND WITH A PURE MINDE

In the beginning of the Scriptures, are to be taught, how the precedent Oration ought to be spoken most secretly, and nothing ought to be retained, which thy Minde and Understanding suggests and prompts to thee in the reading thereof: Then also follow certain words, which are Precepts thereof, which ought always to be begun in the beginning of the Moneth, and also in the dayes. I would also note this, That it is to be pronounced wisely, and with the greatest reverence: and that fasting, before you have taken either Meat or Drink.

## HERE FOLLOWETH THE PRAYER WE SPAKE OF BEFORE, TO OBTAIN A GOOD MEMORY

*O Most Mighty God, Invisible God, Theos Patir Heminas; By thy Archangels, Eliphamasay, Gelonucoa, Gebeche Banai, Gerabcai, Elomnit; and by thy glorious Angels, whose names are so Consecrated, that they cannot be uttered by us; which are these, Do., Hel., X., P., A., Li., O., F, &c. which cannot be comprehended by Humane Sense.*

## HERE FOLLOWING IS THE PROLOGUE OF THE PRECEDENT ORATION, WHICH PROVOKETH AND PROCURETH MEMORY, AND IS CONTINUED WITH THE PRECEDENT NOTE

This Oration ought to be said next to the precedent Oration; to wit, *Lameth*: and with this, I beseech thee today, O *Theos*, to be said always as one continued Oration.

If it be for the Memory, let it be said in the morning; if for any other effect, in the evening.

And thus let it be said in the hour of the evening, and in the morning: And being thus pronounced, with the precedent Oration, it increaseth the Memory, and helpeth the Imperfections of the Tongue.

## HERE BEGINNETH THE PROLOGUE OF THIS ORATION

*I Beseech thee, O my Lord, to Illuminate the Light of my Conscience with the Splendor of thy Light: Illustrate and confirm my Understanding, with the sweet odour of thy Spirit.*

*Adorn my Soul, that hearing I may hear; and what I hear, I may retain in my Memory. O Lord, reform my heart, restore my senses, and strengthen them; qualifie my Memory with thy Gifts: Mercifully open the dulness of my Soul. O most merciful God, temper the frame of my Tongue, by thy most glorious and unspeakable Name: Thou who art the Fountain of all Goodness; the Original and Spring of Piety, have patience with me, give a good Memory unto me, and bestow upon me what I pray of thee in this holy Oration.*

*O thou who dost not forthwith Judge a sinner, but mercifully waitest, expecting his Repentance; I, though unworthy beseech thee to take away the guilt of my sins, and wash away my wickedness and offences, and grant me these my Petitions, by the vertue of thy holy Angels, thou who art one God in Trinity. Amen.*

## HERE HE SHEWETH SOME OTHER VERTUE OF THE PRECEDENT ORATION

If thou doubt of any great Vision, what it may foreshew; or if thou wouldst see any great Vision, of any danger present or to come; or if thou wouldst be certified of any one that is absent, say this Oration three times in the evening with great reverence and devotion, and thou shalt have and see that which thou desireth.

## HERE FOLLOWETH AN ORATION OF GREAT VERTUE, TO ATTAIN THE KNOWLEDGE OF THE PHYSICAL ART, HAVING ALSO MANY OTHER VERTUES AND EFFICACY

If you would have the perfect knowledge of any Disease, whether the same tend to death or life: if the sick party lie languishing, stand before him and say this Oration three times with great reverence.

## THE ORATION OF THE PHYSICAL ART

*Ihesus fili Dominus Incompehensibilis; Ancor, Anacor, Anylos, Zohorna, Theodonos, hely otes Phagor, Norizane, Corichito, Anosae, Helse Tonope, Phagora.*

## ANOTHER PART OF THE SAME ORATION

*Elleminator, Candones helosi, Tephagain, Tecendum, Thaones, Behelos, Belhoros, Hocho Phagan. Corphandonos, Humanaenatus & vos Eloytus Phugora: Be present ye holy Angels, advertise and teach me, whether such a one shall recover, or dye of this Infirmity.*

This being done, then ask the sick person, Friend, how dost thou feel thyself? And if he answer thee, I feel myself at good ease, I begin to mend, or the like; then judge without doubt, the sick person shall recover: but if he answer, I am grievously ill, or worse and worse; then doubtless conclude, He will dye on the morrow: But if he answer, I know not how my Fate and condition is, whether better or worse; then you may know likewise, That he will either dye, or his disease will change and alter for the worse.

If it be a Child, that is not of years capable to make an answer; or that the sick languish so grievously, that he knoweth not how, or will not answer, say this Oration three times; and what you find first revealed in your mind, that judge to come to pass of him.

Furthermore, if anyone dissemble, and seek to hide or cover his infirmity; say the same Oration, and the Angelical Vertue shall suggest the truth to thee. If the diseased person be farre off; when you hear his Name, say likewise this Oration for him, and your minde shall reveal to you, whether he shall live or dye.

If you touch the Pulse of any Woman with Child, saying the same Oration it shall be revealed, whether she shall bring forth a Male or Female.

But know, that this miracle preceeds not from your own Nature, but from the Nature and Vertues of the holy Angels; it being a part of their Office, wonderfully to reveal these things to you. If you doubt of the Virginity of anyone, say this Oration in your mind, and it shall be revealed to you whether she be a Virgin or Corrupt.

## HERE FOLLOWS AN EFFICACIOUS PREFACE OF AN ORATION, SHEWING WHAT VERTUE AND EFFICACY YOU MAY THEREBY PROVE EVERY DAY

Of this Oration Solomon saith, That by it a new knowledge of Physick is to be revealed from God: Upon which, he hath laid this command, and calleth it, The Miraculous and Efficacious Foundation of the Physical Science; and that it containeth in it the quantity and quality of the whole Physical Art and Science: wherein there is contained, rather a miraculous and specious, then fearful or terrible Miracle, which as often-soever as thou readest the same, regard not the paucity of words, but praise the Vertue of so great a Mystery: For, Solomon himself speaking of the subtilty of the Notory Art, wonderfully extolls the Divine Help; to wit, Because we have proposed a great thing, that is to say, so many and so great Mysteries of Nature, contained under so specious brevity, that I suppose them to be as a general Problem to be proposed in the ordination of so subtle and excellent a work; that the mind of the Reader or Hearer may be the more confirmed and fixed here-upon.

HERE HE SHEWETH HOW EVERY NOTE OF EVERY ART OUGHT TO EXERCISE HIS OWN OFFICE; AND THAT THE NOTES OF ONE ART PROFIT NOT TO THE KNOWLEDGE OF ANOTHER ART, AND WE ARE TO KNOW, THAT ALL FIGURES HAVE THEIR PROPER ORATIONS.

We come now, according to our strength, to divide the families of the Notory Art, and leaving that part which is natural, we come to the greater parts of the Art: for Solomon, a great composer, and the greatest Master of the Notory Art, comprehendeth divers Arts under the Notion thereof.

Therefore he calleth this a Notory Art, because it should be the Art of Arts, and Science of Sciences; which comprehendeth in itself all Arts and Sciences, Liberal and Mechanick: And those things which in other Arts are full of long and tedious locutions, filling up great prolixious Volumes of Books, wearying out the Student, through the length of time to attain them: In this Art are comprehended very briefly in a few words or writings, so that it discovereth those things which are hard and difficult making the ingenious learned in a very short time, by the wonderful and unheard-of Vertue of the words.

Therefore we, to whom such a faculty of the knowledge of the Scripture of Sciences is granted, have wholly received this great gift, and inestimable benefit, from the overflowing grace of the most high Creator. And whereas all Arts have their several Notes properly disposed to them, and signified by their Figures; and the Note of every Art, hath not any office of transcending to another Art; neither do the Notes of one Art profit or assist to the knowledge of another Art: Therefore this may seem a little difficult, as this small Treatise, which may be called a Preludium to the Body of the Art: we will explain the Notes severally; and that which is more necessary, we shall by Divine Providence diligently search out the several Sciences of the Scripture.

## A CERTAIN SPECIAL PRECEPT

This is necessary for us, and necessarily we suppose will be profitable to posterity, that we know how to comprehend the great prolixious Volumes of writings, in brief and compendious Treatises; which, that it may easily be done, we are diligently to enquire out the way of attaining to it, out of the three most ancient Books which were composed by Solomon; the first and chiefest thing to be understood therein, is, That the Oration before the second Chapter, it to be used long before every speech, the beginning whereof is Assay: and the words of the Oration are to be said in a competent space of time; but the subsequent part of the Oration is then chiefly to be said, when you desire the knowledge of the Volumes of writings, and looking into the Notes thereof.

The same Oration is also to be said, when you would clearly and plainly understand and expound any Science or great Mystery, that is on a sudden proposed to you, which you never heard of before: say also the same Oration at such time, when any thing of great consequence is importuned of you, which at present you have not the faculty of expounding.

This is a wonderful Oration, whereof we have spoken; the first part whereof is expounded in the Volume of the Magnitude of the quality of Art.

## THE ORATION

*Lamed, Rogum, Ragia, Ragium, Ragiomal, Agaled, Eradioch, Anchovionos, Lochen, Saza, Ya, Manichel, Mamacuo, Lephoa, Bozaco, Cogemal, Saluyel, Tesunanu, Azaroch, Beyestar, Amak.*

To the operation of the Magnitude of Art; this Oration containeth in the second place, a general Treatise of the first Note of all Scripture, part of the Exposition whereof, we have fully explained in the Magnitude of the quality of the same Art.

But the Reader hath hardly heard of the admirable Mystery of the Sacramental Intellect of the same: Let him know this for a certain, and doubt not of the Greek words of the Oration aforesaid, but that the beginning of them is expounded in Latine.

## THE BEGINNING OF THE ORATION

*Oh Eternal and Unreprehensible Memory! Oh Uncontradictible Wisdom! Oh Unchangeable Power! Let thy right-hand encompass my heart, and the holy Angels of thy Eternal Counsel; complete and fill up my Conscience with thy Memory, and the odor of thy Ointments; and let the sweetness of thy Grace strengthen and fortifie my Understanding, through the pure splendor and brightness of thy holy Spirit; by vertue whereof, the holy Angels alwayes behold and admire the brightness of thy face, and all thy holy and heavenly Vertues; Wisdom, wherewith thou hast made all things; Understanding, by which thou hast reformed all things; Perseverance unto blessedness, whereby thou hast restored and confirmed the Angels; Love, whereby thou hast restored lost Mankind, and raised him after his Fall to Heaven; Learning, whereby thou wer't pleased to teach Adam the knowledge of every Science: Inform, repleat, instruct, restore, correct, and refine me, that I may be made new in the understanding thy Precepts, and in receiving the Sciences which are profitable for my Soul and Body, and for all faithful believers in thy Name which is blessed forever, world without end.*

HERE IS ALSO A PARTICULAR EXPOSITION OF THE FORE-GOING ORATION, WHICH HE HATH LEFT UNEXPOUNDED TO BE READ BY EVERYONE THAT IS LEARNED IN THIS ART, AND KNOW, THAT NO HUMANE POWER NOR FACULTY IN MAN IS SUFFICIENT TO FINDE OUT THE EXPOSITION THEREOF

This Oration is also called by Solomon, The Gemme and Crown of the Lord: for he saith, It helpeth against danger of Fire, or of wild Beasts of the Earth, being said with a believing faith: for it is affirmed to have been reported from one of the four Angels, to whom was given power to hurt the Earth, the Sea, and the Trees.

There is an example of this Oration in the Book called, *The Flower of Heavenly Learning*: for herein Solomon glorifieth God, because by this he inspired into him the knowledge of Theologie, and dignified him with the Divine Mysteries of his Omnipotent Power and Greatness: which Solomon beholding in his night-sacrifice, bestowed upon him by the Lord his God, he conveniently gathered the greater Mysteries together in this Notory Art, which were holy, and worthy, and reverend Mysteries. These things and Mysteries of Theologie the erring Gentiles have not all lost, which Solomon calleth, The Signe of the holy Mystery of God revealed by his Angel before; and that which is contained in them, is the fullness of our dignity and humane Salvation.

## THE FIRST OF THESE ORATIONS WHICH WE CALL SPIRITUAL, THE VIRTUE WHERE OF TEACHETH DIVINITY, AND PRESERVETH THE MEMORY THEREOF

These are Orations also, which are of great vertue and efficacy to our Salvation: The first whereof is Spiritual, and teacheth Divinity; and also Perseverance in the Memory thereof: Therefore Solomon commandeth it to be called, The Signe of the Grace of God; for, as Ecclesiastes saith, This is the Spiritual Grace of God, that hath given me knowledge to treat of all Plants, from the Cedar of Lebanon, to the Hyssop that groweth on the wall.

## THE ELECTION OF TIME, IN WHAT LUNATION THESE ORATIONS OUGHT TO BE SAID

The first Oration ought to be said once in the first Lunation; in the third, three times; in the sixth, six times; in the ninth, nine times; in the twelfth, twelve times; in the seventeenth, seventeen times; and in the eighteenth, as many times; in the twenty sixth, as many; in the twenty ninth, as many; and so many in the thirty ninth: for this Oration is of so great vertue and efficacy, that in the very day thou shalt say the same, as if it were determined by the Father, it shall increase thy knowledge in the Science of Divinity.

But if otherwise that thou art ignorant, and it hath been seen by thy Companions, thy Superiors or Inferiors, though unto others thou shalt seem to have knowledge; enter into the study of Divinity, and hear the Lectures by the space of some months, casting off all doubt from thee, of them who shall see thee, to know such things: and in that day wherein thou wouldst say it, live chastly, and say it in the morning.

Solomon testifieth, That an Angel delivered the following Oration in Thunder, who standeth always in the Presence of the Lord, to whom he is not dreadful. The Mystery hereof is holy, and of great efficacy: neither ought this Oration to be said above once, because it moveth the heavenly Spirits to perform any great work.

Of this Oration he saith, That so great is the Mystery thereof, that it moveth the Coelestial Spirits to perform any work which the Divine Power permitteth. It also giveth the vertue of its Mystery, that it exalteth the tongue and body of him that speaketh it, with so great inspiration, as is some new and great Mystery were suddenly revealed to his understanding.

HERE FOLLOWETH THE BEGINNING OF THIS ORATION, WHEREIN IS SO GREAT VIRTUE AND EFFICACY, AS WE HAVE SAID, IT BEING SAID WITH GREAT DEVOTION

*Achacham, Yhel, Chelychem, Agzyraztor, Yegor, &c.*

This is the beginning of the Oration, the parts whereof are four: But there is something to be said of the beginning by itself, and the four parts severally; and then between the beginning and these Orations, which are four, we shall make this competent division.

For this is that which is to be spoken of the beginning severally: And this Oration is to be divided into four parts; and the first part thereof is to be said, that is, the beginning, before any other part of the Oration is to be completed.

These Greek Names following are to be pronounced. This is the division of these Orations,

*Heilma, Helma, Hmena, &c. Oh God the Father, God the Son, God the Holy Spirit, Confirm this Oration, and my Understanding and Memory, to receive, understand, and retain the knowledge of all good Scriptures; and give me perseverance of minde therein.*

This is the beginning of that Oration, which, as we have said before, ought to be said according to the Prolations and Constitutions thereof; and ought to be repeated, because of the forgetfulness of our Memory, and according to the exercise of our wit, and according to the sanctity of our life; there being contained in it so great a Mystery, and such efficacious Vertue.

There followeth another subtle Oration, wherein is contained a Sacramental Mystery, and wherein every perfect Science is wonderfully compleated: For hereby God would have us to know, what things are Celestial, and what are Terrene; and what heavenly things the Celestial effecteth, and what earthly things the Terrene: because the Lord hath said, My eyes have seen the imperfect, and in thy book every day shall be formed and written, and no Man in them, &c.

So it is in the Precepts of God: for we are not able to write all things, how the Sun hath the same course as at first, that our order may be confirmed; for all writings whatsover, which is not from God, is not to be read; for God himself would have all things to be divided: and this is how these are to be used, before the second part, which containeth so glorious and excellent Consecrations of Orations, and defineth the Consecrated part to have no power in the Heavens, and in no wise can be defined by humane Tongues.

## THIS IS THE BEGINNING OF THE SECOND PART OF THAT ORATION SPOKEN OF BEFORE, WHICH IS OF GREAT VIRTUE.

*Aglaros, Theomiros, Thomitos, &c.*

This is the second part of the precedent Oration, of which some singular thing is to bespoken. Whereof if thou sayest this Oration, commemorating the first part thereof, say the Oration following, and thou shalt perceive the precepts which are therein.

*Oh God of all things, who art my God, who in the beginning hast created all things out of nothing, and hast reformed all things by the Holy Spirit; complete and restore my conscience, and heal my understanding, that I may glorify thee in all my works, thoughts and words.*

And after thou hast said this Oration, make a little respite the space of half an hour, and then say the third part of the Oration, which follows:

*Megal, Legal, Chariotos, &c.*

Having said this third part of the Oration, then meditate with thy self about the Scriptures thou desirest to know; and then say this Oration.

*Oh thou that art the Truth, Light, and Way, of all Creatures; Oh Just God, vivify me, and confirm my understanding, and restore my knowledge and conscience unto me, as thou didst unto King Solomon, Amen.*

Commemorating the parts according to that which is laid down, add the Oration following: the other Orations being said, say the fourth part of the Oration, which is this,

*Amasiel, Danyihayr, &c.*

271

## THEN THE PARTS BEING COMMEMORATED AS IS DIRECTED, ADD ALSO THE FOLLOWING ORATION

*I speak these things in thy presence, Oh Lord my God, before whose face all things are naked and open, that I, being washed from the error of infidelity, thy all-quicking Spirit may assist me, and take away all incredulity from me.*

## HOW THE LATINE ORATIONS ARE NOT EXPOUNDED BY THE WORDS OF THE ORATIONS.

For this Oration is such a Mystery, as King Solomon himself witnesseth, that a Servant of his house having found this book by chance, and being too much overcome with Wine in the company of a Woman, he presumtuously read it; but before he had finished a part thereof, he was stricked dumb, blind and lame, and his Memory taken from him; so he continued to the day of his death: and in the hour of his death, he spoke and said, that four Angels which he had offended in presumtuous reading so sacred a mystery, were the daily keepers and afflicters, one of his Memory, another of his speech, a third of his sight, and the fourth of his hearing.

By which Testimony this Oration is so much commended by the same King Solomon, and great is the Mystery thereof: we do greatly require and charge every one, that will say or read it, that he do it not presumptuously; for in presumption is sin; Wherefore let this Oration be said, according as is directed.

We therefore hold it convenient and necessary, to speak something of the general precepts of art, and of the knowledge of all arts; and of the several precepts of every singular art: but because we have touched something of the course of the Moon, it is necessary that we shew what her course signifies. The Moon passeth through 12 Signs in one Moneth; and the Sun through 12 Signs in a year; and in the same term and time, the Spirit inspireth, fruifieth and illustrateth them; whence it is said, that the Sun and the Moon run their course: it is understood the course which first they had. But because this is wanting in the Hebrew, we thought good to omit it in the Latine, having spoken sufficiently of the preceding Oration, and the three parts thereof.

## IN THIS CHAPTER HE SHEWETH THE EFFICACY OF THE SUBSEQUENT ORATION, IT BEING SPECIAL TO OBTAIN ELOQUENCE

This Holy Oration which followeth, is a certain special Oration, to obtain Eloquence; whereas all others have virtue and efficacy in other things, this containeth this certain special mystery in it self: and whereas one of the generals is shewing in it self, certain general precepts, common to all arts; for so God instituted the Soul in the Body, saying; This I give to you, that ye may keep and observe the Law of the Lord; And these are they that stand in the presence of God alwayes, and see their Savior face to face night and day: So of this Oration, I say, This is that most glorious, mystical and intelligible Oration, containing such mysteries in it, which the mind, conscience and tongue succeedeth.

This is such a mystery, that a man shall keep it according to his will, who foreseeth all things in his sight that are made; for the mystery of this Oration is glorious and Sacramental: let no man presume to say any of this Oration after too much drinking or Luxury; nor fasting, without great reverence and discretion.

Whence Solomon saith; Let no man presume to treat anything of this Oration, but in certain determinate and appointed times, unless he make mention of this Oration before some great President, for some weighty business; for which this Oration is of wonderful excellent virtue.

The goodness of this Oration, and the attaining to the effects thereof, it is read in that Psalm wherein it is said, Follow me, and I will make you Fishers of Men, as he said and did.

We know that it is not of our power, that this Oration is of so great Virtue, and such a mystery as sometimes also the Lord said to his Disciples, This we are not able to know: for this Oration is such a mystery, that it containeth in it the great Name of God; which many have lied in saying they knew it; for Jesus himself performed many Miracles in the Temple by it: But many have lyed about what he did, and have hid and abandoned the truth thereof; so that none have declared the same before it came to passe: but we suppose have spoken something about or concerning it.

## IN THIS CHAPTER HE SETTETH DOWN THE TIME AND MANNER HOW THIS ORATION IS TO BE PRONOUNCED

For this Oration is one of the generals, and the first of particulars, containing both in it self; having a special virtue and faculty, to gain Eloquence in it self: therefore it is necessary to be understood what time, ordination, and what dayes it is to be said and published.

It may always be rehearsed in every 14 Lunary as above said; but the ordination of the time for every day, wherein it is to be said, is especially in the morning betimes, before a man is defiled; and then all Orations are chiefly to be said. And this Oration must be then pronounced totally together, without any division. And although there are divisions therein, the Oration is not divided in itself; but only the Divine and Glorious Names are written severally, and are divided into parts, according to the terminations of every great and Glorious name; and it is to be said together as a most excellent name, but not as one Word, because of the fragility of our nature; Neither is it needful to know the Elements of syllables, posited in this Oration; they are not to be known; neither let anyone presumptuously speak them; neither let him do any thing by way of temptation, concerning this Oration, which ought not to be done:

*Elmot, Sehel, Hemech, Zaba, &c*

## NO MAN THAT IS IMPEDITED OR CORRUPTED WITH ANY CRIME OUGHT TO PRESUME TO SAY THIS ORATION

This is a thing agreed unto amongst the wise men of this World, that these things, as we have said before, be pronounced with great reverence and industry: it may be said every day, wherein thou art not hindered by some criminal sin; and in that day wherein thou art impedited by some criminal sin, thou maist remember it in thy heart; and if thou dost desire to be made Eloquent, repeat it three times. And if any evil thing trouble thee, or thou art emerged and involved into any great business, repeat this Oration once, and Eloquence shall be added to thee, as much as is needed; and if thou repeat it over twice, great Eloquence shall be given to thee: so great a Sacrament is this Oration.

The third thing to be considered in this Oration, is; This Oration ought so to be pronounced, that confession of the Heart and Mouth ought to precede it: let it be pronounced in the morning early, and after that Oration say the Latine Oration following.

## THIS IS A PROLOGUE OR EXPOSITION OF THE PRECEDENT ORATION, WHICH OUGHT TO BE SAID TOGETHER

*Oh omnipotent and eternal God, and merciful Father, blessed before all Worlds; who art a God eternal, incomprehensible, and unchangeable, and hast granted this blessed gift of Salvation unto us; according to the omnipotency of thy Majesty, hast granted unto us; the faculty of speaking and learning, which thou hast denied to all other animals; and hast disposed of all things by thy infallible providence: thou art God, whose Nature is eternal and consubstantial, exalted above the Heavens; in whom the whole Deity corporally dwells: I implore thy Majesty, and Glorify thy omnipotency, with an intentive imploration, adoring the mighty Virtue, Power, and Magnificence of thy eternity. I beseech thee, Oh my God, to grant me the inestimable Wisdom of the Life of thy holy Angels. Oh God the Holy Spirit, incomprehensible, in whose presence stand the Holy quires of Angels; I pray and beseech thee, by thy Holy and Glorious Name, and by the sight of thy Angels, and the Heavenly Principalities, to give thy grace unto me, to be present with me, and to give unto me power to persevere in the Memory of thy Wisdom, who livest and reignest eternally one eternal God, through all worlds of worlds; in whose sight are all Celestial Virtues, now and alwayes, and everywhere, Amen.*

This Oration being thus finished, there must of necessity some Mystery be added; so that you are to be silent a while after the Latine Oration is ended: and after a little taciturnity, that is, a little space of silence, begin to say this Oration following seriously:

*Semet, Lamen, &c.*

This (saith Solomon) is the Oration of Orations, and a special experiment, whereby all things, whether generals or particulars, are known fully, efficaciously and perfectly, and are kept in the Memory.

But when thou hast by this Oration attained the Eloquence thou desirest, be sparing thereof, and do not rashly declare those things which thy Tongue suggests and administers to thee; for this is the end of all general Precepts, which are given to obtain Memory, Eloquence, and understanding, All those things which are before delivered, of general precepts, are given as signs how the faculty of attaining to the understanding of the general precepts may be had, which also Solomon calleth Spirituals; and those singular arts have singular virtues and powers.

Having now given a sufficient definition of general precepts; and the Orations are laid down, and the Authority of the Orations unto what they are designed; It is now necessary to set down what is to be done, concerning the singular Orations; because we are now to treat of the several and particular arts, that we may follow the example which our builder and Master hath laid before us; for Solomon saith, before we proceed to the singular Notes and Orations of Arts before noted, there ought to be said a Preludium, which is a beginning or Prologue.

## HOW EVERY SEVERAL ART HATH ITS PROPER NOTE

Before we proceed to the singular precepts of several Arts, it is necessary to discover how every several Art hath a several Note.

## OF THE LIBERAL SCIENCES AND OTHER THINGS, WHICH MAY BE HAD BY THAT ART

The Liberal Arts are seaven, and seaven exceptives, and seaven Mechanicks. The seaven exceptives are comprehended under the seaven liberal: It is manifest what the seaven Liberal Arts are, of which we shall first treat.

The Mechanicks are these, which are adulterately called *Hydromancy, Pyromancy, Nigromancy, Chiromancy, Geomancy, Geonegia,* which is comprehended under *Astronomy* and *Neogia.*

*Hydromancy* is a science of divining by the Water; whereby the Masters thereof judged by the standing or running of the Water. *Pyromancy* is an Experiment of divining by the flaming of the fire; which the ancient Philosophers esteemed of great efficacy. *Nigromancy* is a Sacrifice of dead Animals, whereby the Ancients supposed to know many great Experiments without sin, and to attain to great knowledge: from whence Solomon commandeth that they might read seaven Books of that Art without sin; And that two he accompted Sacriledge, and that they could not read two Books of that Art without sin. But having spoken enough hereof, we proceed to the rest.

## OF THE LIBERAL SCIENCES AND OTHER THINGS WHICH MAY BE HAD THEREBY

There are seaven Liberal Arts, which everyone may learn without sin. For Philosophy is great, containing profound Mysteries in itself: These Arts are wonderfully known.

# HE DECLARETH WHAT NOTES THE THREE FIRST LIBERAL ARTS HAVE

For *Grammar* hath three Notes only, *Dialects* two, and *Rhetorick* four, and every one with open and distinct Orations. But wherefore Grammar hath three, Dialects two, and Rhetorick four; that we know King Solomon himself testifieth and affirmeth; for he saith, And as I was admiring and revolving in my heart and mind, which way, from whom and from whence was this Science, an Angel brought one Book, wherein was written the Figures and Orations, and delivered unto me the Notes and Orations of all Arts, plainly and openly, and told me of them all as much as was necessary: And he explained unto me, as to a Child are taught by certain Elements; some tedious Arts in a great space of time, how that I should have these Arts in a short space of time: Saying unto me, So shalt thou be promoted to every science by the increase of these Virtues.

And when I asked him, Lord, whence and how cometh this? The Angel answered, This is a great Sacrament of the Lord, and of his Will: this writing is by the power of the Holy Ghost, which inspireth, fructifieth and increaseth all knowledge; And again the Angel said, Look Upon these Notes and Orations, at the appointed and determinate times, and observe the times as appointed of God, and no otherwise.

When he had thus said he shewed to King Solomon a Book wherein was written, at what times all these always were to be pronounced and published, and plainly demonstrated it according to the Vision of God: Which things I have heard and seen, did operate in them all, according to the Word of the Lord by the Angel: And so Solomon declareth, it came to pass unto him: But we that come after him, ought to imitate his Authority, as much as we are able to observe those things he hath left unto us.

## HERE SOLOMON SHEWETH HOW THE ANGEL TOLD HIM DISTINCTLY, WHEREFORE THE GRAMMAR HATH THREE FIGURES

Behold wherefore the Grammatical Art hath only three Notes in the Book of Solomon; Gemeliath, that is, in the Book of the Art of God, which we read is the Art of all other Sciences, and of all other Arts; For Solomon saith, When did I inquire everything singularly of the Angel of God, with fear, saying, Lord, from whence shall this come to passe to me, that I may fully and perfectly know this Art? Why do so many Notes appertain to such an Art, and so many to such an Art, and are ascribed to several determinate Orations, to have the efficacy thereof? The Angel is thus said to answer: The Grammatical Art is called a liberal Art, and hath three things necessary thereunto; Ordination of words and times; and in them, of Adjuncts or Figures; Simple, compound and various; and a various declination of the parts to the parts, or a relation from the parts, and a Congruent and ordinate division.

This is the reason, why there is three Notes in the Art of Grammar: And so it pleased the Divine Wisdom, that as there should be a full knowledge of declining by one; by another, that there should be had a convenient Ordination of all the parts; by the third, there should be had a continual and convenient Division of all the parts, simple and compound.

## THE REASON WHY THE DIALECTICAL ART HATH TWO FIGURES ONELY

Dialect, which is called the form of Arts, and a Doctrinal speech, hath two things necessary thereunto, to wit, Eloquence of Arguing, and Prudence to answer; Therefore the greatness of the Divine Providence and Piety, hath appointed two Notes to it; that by the first, we may have Eloquence to Argue and Dispute; and by the second, industry to answer without ambiguity: Wherefore there are ascribed to Grammar three Notes, and to Dialect two Notes

# THE REASON WHY RHETORICK HATH FOUR FIGURES

Let us see wherefore Rhetorick hath four Notes. For there are four things necessary therein; as the Angel of the Lord said unto Solomon; to wit, a continual and flourishing adornment of locution, An ordinate, competent and discreet judgement, a Testimony of Causes or Offices, of Chances & Losses, a composed disposition of buying and selling; An Eloquence of the matters of that Art, with a demonstrative understanding.

Therefore the greatness of God hath appointed to the Art of Rhetorick four Notes, with their Holy and Glorious Orations; as they were reverently sent by the Hand of God; that every Note in that Art aforesaid, might have a several faculty, That the first Note in that Art, might give a continual locution, a competent and florishing adornment thereof: The second, to discern Judgements, just and unjust, ordinate and inordinate, true and false: The third, competently to discover offices and causes: and the fourth giveth understanding and Eloquence in all the operations in this Art, without prolixity. See therefore how in Grammar, Logick, and Rhetorick, the several Notes are disposed in the several Arts.

But of all the other Arts and their Notes, we shall speak in their due place and time, as we find them disposed in the book of the same Solomon.

## AT WHAT TIMES AND HOURS THE NOTES OF THESE THREE LIBERAL ARTS ARE TO BE LOOKED INTO

Now we proceed to shew at what time, and how the Notes of these Arts are to be looked into, and the Orations to be said, to attain to these Arts.

If thou art altogether ignorant of the Grammatical Art, and wouldst have the knowledge thereof: if it be appointed thee of God to do this work of works, and have a firm understanding in this Art of Arts; then know that thou maist not presume to do otherwise than this book commandeth thee; for this book of his shall be thy Master, And this Art of his thy Mistress.

## HOW THE GRAMMATICAL NOTES ARE TO BE LOOKED INTO IN THE FIRST MOON

For in this manner, the Grammatical Notes are to be looked into, and the Orations to be said.

In the dayes when the Moon is in her prime, the first Note is to be looked into 12 times, and the Oration thereof repeated 24 times with Holy reverence; making a little space between, let the Oration be twice repeated at the inspection of every Note, and chiefly abstain from sins: do this from the first day of the Moon to the 14, and from the 14 to the 17.

The first and second Notes are to be looked into 20 times, and the Oration to be repeated 30 times, on the 15 and 17 dayes, using some interval between them, All the three Notes are then everyday to be looked into 12 times, and the Orations are to be repeated 20 times: and thus of the Notes of the Art of Grammar.

But if thou hast read any books of this Art, and desirest perfection therein, do as is commanded; using the general Orations to Increase Memory, Eloquence, understanding and perseverance therein, repeating these above in the due time and hours appointed; lest that going beyond thy precept, thou commitest sin: but when thou dost this, see that it be secret to thy self, and that thou have no looker on but God.

Now we come to the Notes.

# HERE FOLLOWETH THE KNOWLEDGE OF THE NOTES

In the beginning of the inspection of all Notes, fast the first day till the evening, if you can; if thou canst not, then take another hour. This is the Grammatical precept.

## OF THE LOGICAL NOTES

The Dialectical Notes may be used every day, except only in those dayes before told of: The Rhetorical every day, except only three dayes of the Moneth, to wit, ☽ . 11. 17. and 19. And they are forbidden on these dayes, as Solomon testifies, the Notes of all Arts, except the Notes of this Art are offered. These precepts are generally to be observed.

## HOW THE LOGICAL NOTES ARE TO BE INSPECTED, AND THE ORATIONS THEREOF SAID

Know, that the Dialectical Notes are four times to be looked into, and the Orations thereof in that day are 20 times to be repeated, making some respite, and having the books of that Art before your Eyes; and so likewise the books of Rhetorick, when the Notes thereof are inspected, as is appointed. This sufficeth for the knowledge of the 3 Arts.

## HOW WE MUST BEWARE OF OFFENCES

Before we proceed to begin the first Note of the Art of Grammar, something is to be tryed before, that we may have the knowledge of the 1, 2 and 3 Notes.

And you ought first to know, in what the Notes of the Grammatical, Logical, or Rhetorical Art are to be inspected, it being necessary that your greatest intentions be to keep from all offences.

## HOW THE NOTES OUGHT TO BE INSPECTED, AT CERTAIN ELECTED TIMES

This is a special and manifest knowledge, wherewith the Notes of the Grammatical Art are known: how they are to be published, at what times, and with what distinction, is duly and competently manifest; it is spoken already of the publishing and inspection of the Notes and Orations: now we shall digress a little to speak something of the times, it being in part done already.

## HOW DIVERSE MONTHS ARE TO BE SOUGHT OUT IN THE INSPECTION OF THE NOTES

We have spoken already of the tearms of this Art, wherein the Orations are to be read, and the Notes to be looked into: it remaineth to declare how the Lunations of these Orations are to be inspected and found out. But see that you mistake not: yet I have already noted the Lunations, wherein the Notes ought to be looked into, and the Orations rehearsed: But there are some Months, wherein the Lunation is more profitable than others: if thou wouldst operate in Theology or Astronomy, do it in a fiery sign; if Grammar or Logick, in ♊ or ♍ : if Musick or Physick, in ♉ or ♎ ; if Rhetorick, Philosophy, Arithmetick or Geometry, in ♊ or ♋ : for Mathematicks, in ♉ or ♊ : so they are well placed, and free from evil; for all Heavenly Potestates and Chorus of Angels, do rejoyce in their Lunations, and determinate dayes.

## HERE IS MADE MENTION OF THE NOTES OF ALL ARTS

I, Apollonius, following the power of Solomon, having disposed my self to keep his works and observations, as it is spoken in the three Notes of Grammar, so will I observe the times as they are to be observed: But the Orations thereof are not written, but are more fully demonstrated in the following work; for what is written of those three Notes, are not Orations, but Definitions of those Notes, written by the Greek, Hebrew, and Chaldean, and other things which are apprehended by us: For those writings which are not understood in Latine ought not to be pronounced, but on those dayes which are appointed by King Solomon, and in those dayes wherein the Notes are inspected, but on those dayes those Holy writings are always to be repeated: and the Latine, on those dayes wherein the Notes are not inspected.

The Notes of the Logical Art are two: and at what times they are to be published is already shewn in part: more shall hereafter be said of them: now we come first to the rest.

The Latine writings may be published, according to the Antiquity of the Hebrews, except on those dayes we have spoken of: for Solomon saith, See that thou perform all those precepts as they are given: But of the rest that follow, it is to be done otherwise: for when thou seest the first Note of Logick, repeat in thy heart the sign in the first Note, and so in the Notes of all Arts, except those whereof a definition shall be given.

## DEFINITIONS OF SEVERAL ARTS, AND THE NOTES THEREOF

We will give also Definitions of several Arts, as it is in the Book of Solomon; Geometry hath one Note, Arithmetick a Note and a half; Philosophy, with the Arts and Sciences contained therein, hath 7 Species; Theology and Astronomy, with the Sciences in them contained, hath 7 Notes, but they are great and dangerous; not great in the pronunciation, but have great efficacy: Musick hath one Note, and Physick one Note; but they are all to be published and rehearsed in their appointed dayes: But know, that in every day wherein you beholdest the Notes of Theology, Philosophy, or of any Arts contained in them, that thou neither laugh nor play, nor sport; because King Solomon, when he saw the forms of these Notes, having overdrunk himself, God was angry with him, and spoke unto him by his Angel, saying, *Because thou hast despised my sacrament, and Polluted and derided my Holy things; I will take away part of thy Kingdome, and I will shorten the dayes of thy Children.* And the Angel added, *The Lord hath forbid thee to enter into the Temple 80 days, that thou maist repent of thy sin.* And when Solomon wept and besought mercy of the Lord, the Angel answered, *Thy dayes shall he prolonged; nevertheless many evills and iniquities shall come upon thy Children, and they shall be destroyed of the iniquities that shall come upon them.*

At the beginning of a Note, having seen the generals; let the specials be looked into. The word of Solomon is to seek unto God for his promises, before the Notes of the three Arts.

## THE FIRST ORATION AT THE BEGINNING OF THE NOTE

*The Light, Truth, Life, Way, Judge, Mercy, Fortitude and Patience, preserve, help me, and have Mercy upon me, Amen.*

This Oration, with the preceding ought to be said in the beginning of the first Note of Grammar.

*Oh Lord, Holy Father, Almighty, eternal God, in whose sight are all the foundations of all creatures, and invisible beings whose Eyes behold my imperfections, of the sweetness of whose love the Earth and Heavens are filled; who sawest all things before they were made, in whose book every day is formed, and all mankind are written therein: behold me, thy Servant this day prostrate me before thee, with thy whole Heart and Soul: by thy Holy Spirit confirm me, blesse me, protect all my Actions in this inspection or repetition, and illuminate me of thy visitation.*

The third Oration: This Oration ought to be said before the second Note of Grammar.

*Behold, O Lord, merciful Father all things, eternal dispensor of all virtues, and consider my operations this day; Thou art the Beholder and Discerner of all the Actions of Men and Angels: Let the wonderful grace of thy promises condescend to fufil this sudden virtue in me, and infuse such efficacy into me, operating in thy Holy and great Name, thou who infusest thy praise into the mouths of them that love thee, Amen.*

The fourth Oration; Let this Oration be rehearsed before the third Grammatical Note:

*O ADONAY, Creator of all visible Creatures! OH most Holy Father, who dwellest incompassed about with eternal light, disposing and by thy power governing all things before all beginnings; I most humbly beseech thy eternity and thy incomprehensible goodness may come to perfection in me, by the operation of thy most Holy Angels; and be confirmed in my Memory, and establish these, thy Holy works in me, Amen.*

A little space after this Oration, say the following: the first Oration ought to be said before the first Note of Logick.

*O Holy God, great good and the eternal Maker of all things, thy Attributes not to be expressed, who hast Created the Heaven and the Earth, the Sea and all things in them, and the bottomless pit according to thy pleasure; in whose sight are the Words and Actions of all men: Grant unto me, by these Sacramental Mysteries of thy Holy Angels, the precious knowledge of this art, which I desire by the Ministery of thy Holy Angels, it being without any Malignant or Malicious intent, Amen.*

Pronounce this Oration in the beginning of the first Figure of the Logick Art; and after this Oration rehearse incontinently with some interval, the Orations written between the first Figure.

The sixth Oration ought to be said before the first Note of the Dialect;

*Helay: Most Merciful Creator, Inspirer, Reformer, and Approver of all Divine Wills, Ordainer of all things, Mercifully give ear to my Prayer, gloriously intend unto the desires of my heart, that what I humbly desire, according to thy promises, thou wilt Mercifully grant, Amen.*

This Oration following, ought to be pronounced before the first Note of the Rhetorical Art:

*Omnipotent and merciful Father, Ordainer and Creator of all Creatures: O most Holy Judge, eternal King of Kings, and Lord of Lords; who wonderfully condescendest to give wisdom and understanding to the Saints, who judgest and discernest all things: I beseech thee to illuminate my heart this day with the Splendor of thy Beauty, that I may understand and know what I desire, and what things are considerable to be known in this Art, Amen.*

This Oration , with the following *Hanazay, &c.* ought to be pronounced before the first Figure of Rhetorick and although the they are divided only the this cause, that there might be some mean interval used in the pronouncing of them; and they ought to be pronounced before the other Orations written in the Figure.

*Hanazay, Sazhaon, Hubi, Sene, Hay, Ginbar, Ronail, Selmore, Hyramay, Lobal, Yzazamael, Amathomatois, Yaboageyors, Sozomcrat, Ampho, Delmedos, Geroch, Agalos, Meihatagiel, Secamai, Sabeleton, Mechogrisces, Lerirenorbon.*

The 8 Oration, let it be pronounced before the second Note of the Rhetorical Art:

*Oh great eternal and wonderful Lord God, who of thy eternal counsel hast disposed of all virtues, and art Ordainer of all goodness; Adorn and beautify my understanding, and give unto me Reason to know and learn the Mysteries of thy Holy Angels: And grant unto me all knowledge and learning thou hast promised to thy Servants by the virtue of thy Holy Angels, Amen.*

This Oration, with the other two following, ought to be pronounced (viz. *Vision, &c.*) *Azelechias, &c.*, in the beginning of the second Figure of Rhetorick, and before the other Orations; and there ought to be some interval between them.

Let this Oration following be said, before the second Note of Rhetorick *Vision;*

*beholding with thy eternal conspiration all Powers, Kingdoms and Judges, Administering all manner of Languages to all, and of whose power there is no end; restore I beseech thee, and increase my Memory, my heart and understanding, to know, understand, and judge all things which thy Divine Authority commendeth necessary in this art, perfectly fulfill them in me, Amen.*

Let this Oration following, with the precedent, be rehearsed before the second Note of Rhetorick.

*Azelechias, Velozeos, Inoanzama, Samelo, Hotens, Sagnath, Adonay, Soma, Jezoehos, Hicon, Jezomethon, Sadaot. And thou Oh God propitiously confirm thy promises in me, as thou hast confirmed them by the same words to King Solomon; send unto me, Oh Lord, thy virtue from Heaven, that may illuminate my mind and understanding: strengthen, Oh God, my understanding, renew my Soul within me, and wash me with the Waters which are above the Heavens; pour out thy Spirit upon my flesh, and fill my bowels with thy Judgements, with humility and charity: thou who hast created Heaven and the Earth, and made Man according to thy own Image; pour out the light of thy love into my understanding, that being radicated and established in thy love and thy mercy, I may love thy Name, and know and worship thee, and understand all thy Scriptures, And all the Mysteries which thou hast declared by thy Holy Angels, I may receive and understand in my Heart, and use this Art to thy Honor and Glory, through thy mighty Counsel, Amen.*

The 11 Oration ought to be said before the pronounciation of the third Note of Rhetorick.

*I know, that I love thy Glory, and my delight is in thy wonderful works, and that thou wilt give unto me wisdome, according to thy goodness and thy power, which is incomprehensible: Theon, Haltanagon, Haramalon, Zamoyma, Chamasal, Jeconamril, Harionatar, Jechomagol, Gela Magos, Kemolihot, Kamanatar, Hariomolatar, Hanaces, Velonionathar, Azoroy, Jezabali; by these most Holy and Glorious profound Mysteries, precious Offices, virtue and knowledge of God, complete and perfect my beginnings and reform my beginnings, Zembar,*

*Henoranat, Grenatayl, Samzatam, Jecornazay: Oh thou great Fountain of all goodness, knowledge and virtue, given unto thy Servant power to eschew all evil, and cleave unto goodness and knowledge, and to follow the same with an Holy intention, that with my whole heart I may understand & learn thy Laws and Decrees; especially these Holy Mysteries; wherein that I may profit, I beseech thee, Amen.*

12. This Oration ought to be said before the ninth Rhetorical Note:

*O most reverend Almighty Lord, ruling all Creatures both Angels and Archangels, and all Celestial, Terrestrial, and Infernal Creatures; of whose greatness comes all plenty, who hast made man after thy own Image; Grant unto me the knowledge of this Art, and strengthen all Sciences in me, Amen.*

13. Pronounce this before the first Figure of Arithmetick:

*Oh God who numbrest, weighest, and measurest all things, given the day his order, and called the Sun by his name; Grant the knowledge of this Art unto my understanding, that I may love thee, and acknowledge the gift of thy goodness, Amen.*

14. Say this before the semi-note of Arithmetick:

*Oh God, the Operator of all things, from whom proceeds every good and perfect gift; sow the Seeds of thy Word in my Heart, that I may understand the excellent Mysteries of this Art, Amen.*

15. Say this before the second Figure of Arithmetick:

*Oh God the perfect Judge of all good works, who maketh known they saving goodness among all Nations; open my Eyes and my heart, with the beams of thy mercy, that I may understand and persever, in these thy Heavenly Mysteries, Amen.*

16. This Oration before the second Note of Geometry:

*Oh God, the giver of all wisdome and knowledge to them that are without sin, Instructor and Master of all Spiritual learning, by thy Angels and Arch-Angels, by Thrones, Potestates, Principates and Powers, by Cherubim and Seraphim, and by the 24 Elders, by the 4 Animals, and all the host of Heaven, I adore, invocate, worship and glorify thy Name, and exalt thee: most terrible and most merciful, I do humbly beseech thee this day to illuminate and fill my Heart with the grace of thy Holy Spirit, thou who art three in one, Amen.*

17. Say this Oration before the second Note on Theology

*I adore thee, O King of Kings, my light, my substance, my life, my King, and my God, my Memory, and my strength; who in a Moment gavest sundry Tongues, and threwest down a Mighty Tower, and gavest by thy Holy Spirit the knowledge of Tongues to thy Apostles, infusing thy knowledge into them in a Moment, giving them the understanding of all Languages: inspire my Heart, and pour the dew of thy grace and Holy Spirit into me, that I may understand the Exposition of Tongues and Languages, Amen.*

THREE CHAPTERS TO BE PUBLISHED, BEFORE ANY OF THE NOTES

What we have spoken of the three first Chapters are generally and specially to be pronounced, so that you say them, and the Orations on the dayes appointed, and work by the Notes as it is demonstrated to you.

These Orations ought to be said alwayes before noon, every day of the Moneth; and before the Notes say the proper Orations: and in all reading, observe the precepts commanded.

## HOW THE PROPER NOTES ARE TO BE INSPECTED

If you would learn anything of one Art, look into the proper Notes thereof in their due time. Enough as said already of the three liberal Arts.

## WHAT DAYS ARE TO BE OBSERVED IN THE INSPECTION OF THE NOTES OF THE FOUR ARTS

In the four other Arts, only the first dayes are to be observed: The Philosophical Notes, with all Sciences contained therein, the 7 and 17 dayes of the Moon are to be inspected, 7 times a day, with their several Orations. The Note is to be looked into, with fear, silence and trembling.

Of the Notes of the liberal Arts, it is spoken already; but only know this, that when you would use them, live chaste and soberly; for the Note hath in itself 24 Angels, is fully and perfectly to be pronounced, as you have heard: but when you look into them, repeat all the Theological Orations, and the rest in their due time.

## OF THE INSPECTION OF GENERAL NOTES

Say the general Notes 10 times a day, when you have occasion to use any common Arts, having the books of those Arts before you, using some interval or space of time between them, as you have been taught already.

## HOW THE THREE FIRST CHAPTERS ARE TO BE PRONOUNCED BEFORE ORATIONS

To have perfection herein, know, that in the general pronounciation of Orations, the Notes of the three heads are to be rehearsed; whether the Orations be pronounced or not.

## HOW THE FIFTH ORATION OF THEOLOGY OUGHT TO BE REHEARSED UPON THESE ORATIONS

There is also something else to be said of the four other liberal Arts; if you would have the perfect knowledge of them, make the first Oration of Theology before you say the Orations of the other Notes.

These are sufficiently declared, that you might understand and know them; And let the capitular Orations be pronounced before the several Notes of every Art, and kept as is determined, &c.

These are the Augmentations of the Orations, which belong to all Arts, liberal and exceptive, except Mechanick, and are especially ascribed to the Notes of Theology. And they are thus to be pronounced, that whensoever you look into any one Note of any Art, and would profit therein, say these Orations following.

1. *Ezamamos, Hazalat, Ezityne, Hezemechel, Czemomechel, Zamay, Zaton, Ziamy Nayzaton, Hyzemogoy, Jeccomantha, Jaraphy, Phalezeton, Sacramphal, Sagamazaim, Secranale, Sacramathan, Jezennalaton Hacheriatos, Jetelemathon, Zaymazay, Zamaihay Gigutheio Geurlagon, Garyos. Mega'on Hera Cruhic, Crarihuc, Amen.*

Let this Oration with the following be pronounced before the first Note of Philosophy:

*Oh Lord God, Holy Father, Almighty and incomprehensible; hear my Prayers, thou that art invisible, immortal and intelligible, whose face the Angels and Arch-Angels, and all the powers of Heaven, do so much desire to see; whose Majesty I desire eternally to adore, and honor the only one God for ever and ever. Amen.*

2. Say this before the second Note of Philosophy:

*Oh Lord God, Holy and Almighty Father, hear my Prayers this day, and incline thy ears to my Orations; Gezomelion Samach, Semath, Cemon, Gezagam, Gezatrhin, Zheamoth, Zeze Hator Sezeator Samay Sannanda, Gezyel, Iezel, Gaziety, Hel, Gazayethyhel, Amen.*

Say this following with the former:

*Oh God eternal, the way, the truth, and the life; give thy light and the flower of thy Holy Spirit into my mind and understanding, and grant that the gift of thy grace may shine forth in my heart, and into my Soul, now and forever, Amen.*

3. Pronounce the Oration following before the third Note of Philosophy;

*Lemogethom, Hegemochom, Hazachay Hazatha, Azamachar, Azacham, Cohathay, Geomothay Logomothay, Zathana, Lachanma, Legomezon, Legornozon, Lembdemachon, Zegomaday, Haihanayos, Hatamam, Helesymom, Vagedaren, Vadeyabar, Lamnanath, Lamadai, Gomongchor, Gemecher, Ellemay, Gecromal, Gecrohahi, Colomanos, Colomaythos, Amen.*

Say this Oration following with the precedent Oration:

*Oh God the life of all visible Creatures, eternal brightness, and virtue of all things; who art the original of all piety, who knewest all thing before they were; who judgest all things, and discerneth all things by the unspeakable knowledge: glorify thy Holy and unspeakable Name this day in my heart, and strengthen my intellectual understanding; increase my Memory, and confirm my eloquence; make my tongue ready, quick, and perfect in thy Sciences and Scriptures, that by thy power given unto me, and thy wisdome taught in my heart, I may praise thee, and know and understand thy Holy Name for ever World without end, Amen.*

4. Say this Oration following before the fourth Note of Philosophy:

*Oh King of Kings, the Giver and Dispenser of infinite Majesty, and of infinite mercy, the founder of all foundations; lay the foundation of all thy virtues in me, remove all foolishness from my heart, that my senses may be established in the love of thy charity, and my Spirit informed by thee, according to the recreation and invocation of thy will, who livest and reignest God throughout all Worlds of Worlds, Amen.*

## HOW THESE ORATIONS ARE TO BE SAID EVERY DAY ONCE BEFORE THE GENERAL NOTE, AND THE NOTES OF THE LIBERAL ARTS

These 4 Orations are necessary for liberal Arts, but chiefly do appertain to Theology, which are to be said every day before the general Notes, or the Notes of the liberal Arts; but to Theology say every one of these 7 times to every Note; but if you would learn or teach anything of dictating, versifying, singing or Musick, or any of these Sciences, first teach him these Orations, that thou wouldst teach, how he should read them: but if he be a Child of mean understanding, read them before him, and let him say after thee word for word; but if he be of a good understanding, let him read them 7 times a day for 7 days: or if it be a general Note, pronounce these Orations, and the Virtue thereof shall profit you much, and you shall therein find great virtue.

Solomon saith of these Orations, Let no man presume to make use of them unless for the proper Office they are instituted for.

5. *Oh Father, incomprehensible, from whom proceedeth everything that is good; whose greatness is incomprehensible: hear this day my Prayers, which I make in thy sight, and grant to me the Joy of thy saving health, that I may teach unto the wicked the wayes and Paths of thy Sciences, and convert the Rebellious & incredulous unto thee, that whatsoever I commemorate and repeat in my heart and mouth, may take root and foundation in me; that I may be made powerful and efficacious in thy works, Amen.*

6. Say this Oration before the 6 Note of Philosophy;

*Gezemothon, Oronathian, Heyatha, Aygyay, Lethasihel, Iaechizliet, Gerohay, Gerhomay, Sanoaesorel, Sanasathel, Gissiomo, Hatel, Segomasay, Azomathon, Helomathon, Gerochor, Hojazay, Samin, Heliel, Sanihelyel, Siloth, Silerech, Garamathal, Gesemathal, Gecoromay, Gecorenay, Samyel, Samihahel, Hesemyhel, Sedolamax, Secothamay, Samya, Rabiathos, Avinosch, Annas, Amen.*

Then say the following:

*Oh eternal King! O God, the Judge and discerner of all things, knower of all good Sciences; instruct me this day for thy Holy Names sake, and by these Holy Sacraments; and purify my understanding, that thy knowledge may enter into my inward parts, as water flowing from Heaven, and as Oil into my bones, by thee, Oh God Saviour of all things, who art the fountain of goodness, and original of piety; instruct me this day in those Holy Sciences which I desire, thou who art one God for ever, Amen.*

*Oh God Father, incomprehensible, from whom preceedeth all good, the greatness of whose mercy is fathomless, hear my Prayers, which I make this day before thee, and render unto me the joy of thy Salvation, that I may teach the unjust the knowledge of thy wayes, and convert the unbelieving and Rebellious unto thee; and may have power to perform thy works, Amen.*

HOW THESE ORATIONS ARE TO BE SAID EVERY DAY ONCE BEFORE
THE GENERAL NOTE, AND THE NOTES OF THE LIBERAL ARTS

7. *Oh God of all piety, Author and Foundation of all things, the eternal Health and Redemption of thy People; Inspirer and great Giver of all graces, Sciences and Arts, from whose gift it cometh: Inspire into me thy servant, an increase of those Sciences: who hast granted life to me miserable sinner, defend my Soul, and deliver my Heart from the wicked cogitations of this World; extinguish and quench in me the flames of all lust and fornication, that I may the more*

attentively delight in thy Sciences and Arts; and give unto me the desire of my Heart, that I being confirmed and exalted in thy Glory, may love thee: and increase in me the power of thy Holy Spirit, by thy Salvation and reward of the faithful, to the Salvation of my Soul and Body, Amen.

Then say this following:

Oh God, most mighty Father, from whom proceedeth all good, the greatness of whose mercy is incomprehensible; hear my Prayers, that I make in thy sight.

## SPECIAL PRECEPTS OF THE NOTES OF THEOLOGY, CHIEFLY OF THE 1. 2. AND 3

These 7 Orations are to be an augmentation of the rest, and ought to be said before all the Notes of Theology, but especially before the ineffable Note; these are the precepts to make thee sufficient, which we command thee to observe by the authority of Solomon: diligently inquire them out, and do as we have proposed, and perfectly pronounce the Orations, and look into the Notes of the other Arts.

## HOW SOLOMON RECEIVED THAT INEFFABLE NOTE FROM THE ANGEL

Because thou desirest the Mystery of the Notes, take this of the ineffable Note, the expression whereof is given in the Angels by the Figures of Swords, birds, trees, Flowers, Candles and Serpents; for Solomon received this from the Lord in the night of Pacification, ingraven in a book of Gold; and heard this from the Lord: Doubt not, neither be affraid; for this Sacrament is greater then all the rest; And the Lord joyned it unto him, When thou look'st into this Note and read'st the Orations thereof, observe the precepts before, and diligently look into them; And beware that thou prudently conceal and keep whatsoever thou read'st in this Note of God, and whatsoever shall be revealed to thee in the vision.

And when the Angel of the Lord appeareth to thee, keep and conceal the words and writings he revealeth to thee; and observe them to practice and operate in them, observing all things with great reverence, and pronounce them at the appointed dayes and hours, as before is directed; and afterwards say;

*Sapienter die illo; Age, & caste vivas.*

But if thou dost anything uncertain, there is danger; as thou wilt have experience from the other Notes and Orations of them, but consider that which is most wonderful in those Orations; for these words are ineffable Names, and are spiritually to be pronounced before the ineffable Note,

*Hosel, Jesel, Anchiator, Aratol, Hasiatol, Gemor, Gesameor.*

Those are the Orations which ought to be pronounced after the inspection of all the Arts, and after the Note of Theology.

This is the fulfilling of the whole work; but what is necessary for an experiment of the work, we will more plainly declare. In the beginning of the knowledge of all Arts there is given almost the perfect Doctrine of operating: I say almost, because some flourishing institutions hereof remain, whereof this is the first beginning.

## HOW THE PRECEPTS ARE TO BE OBSERVED IN THE OPERATION OF ALL ARTS

Observe the 4 ☽ in every operation of Theology. Exhibit that operation with efficacy every 4 ☽ quartram lunam; and diligently look into the books and writings of those Arts; if thou doubt of any of the Chapters, they are to be pronounced, as is taught of the superior Chapters; but know this, that these Holy Words of Orations, we appoint to be said before the bed of the sick, for an experiment of life or death.

And this thou maist do often, if thou wil to perate nothing else in the whole body of Art: And know this; that if thou hast not the books in thy hands, or the faculty of looking into them is not given to thee; the effect of this work will not be the lesse therefore: but the Orations are twice then to be pronounced, where they were to be but once: And as to the knowledge of a vision, and the other virtues which these Holy Orations have; thou maist prove and try them, when and how thou wilt.

## THESE PRECEPTS ARE SPECIALLY TO BE OBSERVED

But when thou would'st operate in Theology, observe only those dayes which are appointed; but all times are convenient for those Notes and Orations, for which there is a competent time given; but in the pronounciation of the three liberal Arts, or in the inspection of their Notes, perhaps thou maist pretermit some day appointed, if thou observe the rest; or if thou transgress two dayes, leave not off the work, for it loseth not its effect for this, for the Moon is more to be observed in the greater numbers than the dayes or hours. For Solomon saith, If thou miss a day or two, fear not, but operate on the general Chapters.

This is enough to say of them: but by no means forget any of the words which are to be said in the beginning of the reading to attain to Arts; for there is great virtue in them. And thou maist frequently use the Holy Words of the visions: but if thou wouldst operate in the whole body of the Physical Art, the first Chapters are first to be repeated as before are defined. And in Theology, thou must operate only by thy self: Often repeat the Orations, and look into the Notes of Theology: this produceth great effects. It is necessary that thou have the Note of the 24 Angels always in Memory; and faithfully keep those things, which the Angel reveales to thee in the vision.

## THE EXPERIMENT OF THE PRECEDENT WORK, IS THE BEGINNING OF THE FOLLOWING ORATIONS, WHICH SOLOMON CALLETH ARTEM NOVAM

These Orations may be said before all Arts generally, and before Notes specially; and they may be pronounced without any other Chapters, if thou wouldst operate in any of the aforesaid Arts, saying these Orations in due time and order; thou maist have great efficacy in any Art.

And in saying these Orations, neither the time, day, nor Moon, are to be observed: but take heed, that on these dayes you abstain from all sin, as drunkenness, gluttony, especially swearing, before you proceedeth thereunto, that your knowledge therein may be the more clear and perfect.

Wherefore Solomon saith, When I was to pronounce these Orations, I feared lest I should offend God; and I appointed unto myself a time wherein to begin them; that living chastly, I might appear the more innocent.

These are the Proemiums of these Orations, that I might lay down in order everything whereof thou maist doubt, without any definition. And before thou begin to try any of these subtle works, it is good to fast two or three dayes; that is may be Divinely revealed, whether thy desires be good or evil.

These are the precepts appointed before every operation; but if thou doubt of any beginning, either of the three first Chapters, or of the four subsequent Arts, that thou maist have the effect of perfect knowledge; if thou consider and pronounce these Orations, as they are above described, although thou overpass something ignorantly; thou maist be reconciled by the spiritual virtue of the subsequent Orations

The Angel said of these Orations to Solomon: See the Holiness of these Orations; and if thou hast transgrest any therein presumtuously or ignorantly, say reverently and wisely these Orations, of which the Angel saith: *This is a great Sacrament of God, which the Lord sendeth to thee by my hand;* at the veneration of which Sacrament, when King Solomon offered with great patience before the Lord upon the Alter, he saw the book covered with fine linen, and in this book were written 10 Orations, and upon every Oration the sign of a golden Seal: and he heard in his Spirit, These are they which the Lord hath figured, and are far excluded from the hearts of the unfaithful.

Therefore Solomon trembled, lest he should offend the Lord, and kept them, saying it was wickedness to reveal them to unbelievers: but he that would learn any greater spiritual thing in any Art or necessary Science, if he cannot have a higher work, he may say these Orations at what time soever he will; the three first, for the three first liberal Arts; a several Oration for every several Art, or generally all of the three for the three Arts are to be said; and in like manner the four subsequent Orations, for four other liberal Arts.

And if thou wouldst have the whole body of Art, without any definition of time, thou maist pronounce these Orations before the several Arts, and before the Orations and Notes of these Arts, as often as thou wilt, manifestly and secretly; but beware that thou live chastly and soberly in the pronounciation thereof.

This is the first Oration of the 10, which may be pronounced by its self, without any precedent work to acquire Memory, Eloquence and understanding, and stable×ness of these three, and singularly to be rehearsed before the first Figure of Theology:

*Omnipotent, Incomprehensible, invisible and indissolvable Lord God; I adore this day thy Holy Name; I, an unworthy and miserable sinner, do lift up my Prayer, understanding and reason towards thy Holy and Heavenly Temple, declaring thee, O Lord God, to be my Creator and Savior: and I, a rational Creature do this day Invocate thy most glorious clemency, that thy Holy Spirit may vivify my infirmity: And thou, Oh my God, who didst confer the Elements of letters, and efficacious Doctrine of thy Tongue to thy Servants Moses and Aaron, confer the same grace of thy sweet✕ness upon me, which thou hast investigated into thy Servants and Prophets: as thou hast given them learning in a moment, confer the same learning upon me, and cleanse my Conscience from dead works; direct my Heart into the right way, and open the same to understand, and drop truth into my understanding, And thou, Oh Lord God, who didst condescend to create me in thy own image, hear me in thy Jus✕tice, and teach me in thy truth, and fill up my Soul with thy knowledge according to thy great mercy, that in the multitude of thy mercies, thou maist love me the more, and the greater in thy works, and that I may delight in the administration of thy Commandments; that I being helped and restored by the work of thy grace, and purified in Heart and Conscience to trust in thee, I may feast in thy sight, and exalt thy Name, for it is good, before thy Saints: Sanctifie me this day, that I may live in faith, perfect in hope, and constant in charity, and may learn and obtain the knowl✕edge I desire; and being illuminated, strengthened and exalted by the Science obtained, I may know thee, and love thee, and love the knowledge and wisdome of the Scriptures; and that I may understand and firmly retain, that which thou hast permitted Man to know: Oh Lord Jesus Christ, eternal only begotten Son of God, into whose hands the Father gave all thing before all Worlds, give unto me this day, for thy Holy and glorious Name, the unspeakable nutriment of Soul and Body, a fit, fluent, free and perfect Tongue; and that whatsoever I shall ask in thy mercy, will and truth, I may obtain; and confirm all my Prayers and actions, according to thy good pleasure. Oh Lord my God, the Father of Life, open the Fountain of Sciences, which I desire; open to me, Oh Lord, the Fountain which thou openest to Adam, and to thy Servants Abraham, Isaac, and Jacob, to understand, learn and judge; receive Oh Lord my Prayers, through all thy Heavenly virtues, Amen.*

The next Oration is the second of ten, and giveth Eloquence, which ought to be said after the other; a little interval in between, and before the first Figure of Theology.

*I Adore thee, thou King of Kings, and Lords, eternal and unchangeable King: Hearken this day to the cry and sighing of my Heart and Spirit, that thou maist change my understanding, and give to me a heart of flesh, for my heart of stone, that I may breathe before my Lord and Savior; and wash Oh Lord with thy new Spirit the inward parts of my heart, and wash away the evil of my flesh: infuse into me a good understanding, that I may become a new man; reform me in thy love, and let thy salvation give me increase of knowledge: hear my Prayers, O Lord, wherewith I cry unto thee, and open the Eyes of my flesh, and understanding, to understand the wonderful things of thy Law; that being vivified by thy Justification, I may prevail against the Devil, the adversary of the faithful; hear me Oh Lord my God, and be merciful unto me, and shew me thy mercy; and reach to me the vessel of Salvation, that I may drink and be satisfied of the Fountain of thy grace, that I may obtain the knowledge and understanding; and let the grace of thy Holy Spirit come, and rest upon me, Amen.*

## FOR ELOQUENCE AND STABILITY OF MIND

This is the third Oration of the ten, and is to be said before the first Figure of Astronomy.

*I confesse my self guilty this day before thee Oh God, Father of Heaven and Earth, Maker of all things, visible and invisible, of all Creatures, Dispenser and giver of all grace and virtue; who hidest wisdome and knowledge from the proud and wicked, and givest it to the faithful and humble; illuminate my Heart, and establish my Conscience and understanding: set the light of thy countenance upon me, that I may love thee, and be established in the knowledge of my understanding, that I being cleansed from evil works, may attain to the knowledge of those Sciences, which thou hast reserved for believers.*

*Oh merciful and Omnipotent God, cleanse my Heart and reins, strengthen my Soul and Senses with the grace of thy Holy Spirit, and establish me with the fire of the same grace: illuminate me; gird up my loyns, and give the staffe of thy Consolation into my right hand, direct me in thy Doctrine; root out of me all vices and sin, and comfort me in the love of thy mercies: Breathe into me, Oh Lord, the breath of Life, and increase my reason and understanding; send thy Holy Spirit into me, that I may be perfect in all knowledge: behold Oh Lord, and consider the dolour of my mind, that my wil may be comforted in thee; send into me from Heaven thy Holy Spirit, that I may understand those things I desire.*

*Give unto me invention, Oh Lord, thou Fountain of perfect reason and riches of knowledge, that I may obtain wisdom by thy Divine assistance, Amen.*

## TO COMFORT THE OUTWARD AND INWARD SENSES

*Oh Holy God, mercyful and omnipotent Father, Giver of all things; strengthen me by thy power, and help me by thy presence, as thou wert mercyful to Adam, and suddenly gavest him the knowledge of all Arts through thy great mercy; grant unto me power to obtain the same knowledge by the same mercy: be present with me Oh Lord, and instruct me: : Oh most merciful Lord Jesus Christ, Son of God, breathe thy Holy Spirit into me, proceeding from thee and the Father; strengthen my work this day, and teach me, that I may walk in thy knowledge, and glorify the abundance of thy grace: Let the flames of thy Holy Spirit rejoyce the City of my Heart, by breathing into me thy Divine Scriptures; replenish my Heart with all Eloquence, and vivify me with thy Holy visitation; blot out of me the spots of all vices, I beseech thee, Oh Lord God incomprehensible; let thy grace always be rest upon me, and be increased in me; heal my Soul by thy inestimable goodness, and comfort my heart all my life, that what I hear I may understand, and what I understand I may keep, and retain in my Memory; give me a teachable Heart and Tongue; through thy inexhaustible grace and goodness; and the grace of the Father, Son, and Holy Ghost, Amen.*

## THIS FOLLOWING IS FOR THE MEMORY

*O Holy Father, merciful Son, and Holy Ghost, inestimable King; I adore, invocate, and beseech thy Holy Name that of thy overflowing goodness, thou wilt forget all my sins: be mercyful to me a sinner, presuming to go about this office of knowledge, and occult learning; and grant, Oh Lord, it may be efficatious in me; open Oh Lord, my ears, that I may hear; and take away the scales from my Eyes, that I may see; strengthen my hands, that I may work; open my face, that I may understand thy will; to the glory of thy Name, which is blessed forever, Amen.*

## THIS FOLLOWING STRENGTHENETH THE INTERIOR AND EXTERIOR SENSES

*Lift up the senses of my Heart and Soul unto thee, Oh Lord my God, and elevate my heart this day unto thee; that my words and works may please thee in the sight of all people; let thy mercy and omnipotency shine in my bowels: let my understanding be enlarged, and let thy Holy Eloquence be sweet in my mouth, that what I read or hear I may understand and repeat: as Adam understood, and as Abraham kept, so let me keep understanding; and as Jacob was founded and rooted in thy wisdom, so let me be: let the foundation of thy mercy be confirmed in me, that I may delight in the works of thy hands, and persevere in Justice, and peace of Soul and Body; the grace of thy Holy Spirit working in me, that I may rejoyce in the overthrow of all my adversaryes, Amen.*

## THIS FOLLOWING GIVETH ELOQUENCE, MEMORY AND STABILITY

*Disposer of all Kingdomes, and of all visible and invisible gifts: Oh God, the Ordainer and Ruler of all wills, by the Counsel of thy Holy Spirit dispose and vivify the weakness of my understanding, that I may burn in the accesse of thy Holy will to good: do good to me in thy good pleasure, not looking upon my sins; grant me my desire, though unworthy; confirm my Memory and reason to know, understand, and retain, and give good effect to my sense through thy grace, and justify me with the justification of thy Holy Spirit, that what spots soever of sin are contracted in my flesh, thy Divine power may blot out; thou who hast been pleased in the beginning, to create the Heaven and the Earth, of thy mercy restore the same, who art pleased to restore lost man to thy most Holy Kingdome; Oh Lord of wisdome, restore Eloquence into all my senses, that I, though an unworthy sinner, may be confirmed in thy knowledge, and in all thy works, by the grace of the Father, Son, and Holy Ghost, who livest and reignest three in one, Amen.*

## AN ORATION TO RECOVER LOST WISDOM

*Oh God of the living, Lord of all Creatures visible and invisible, Administrator and Dispenser of all things, enlighten my Heart this day by the grace of thy Holy Spirit, strengthen my inward man, and pour into me the dew of thy grace, whereby thou instructest the Angels; inform me with the plenty of thy knowledge, wherewith from the beginning thou hast taught thy faithful; let thy grace work in me, and the flouds of thy grace and Spirit, cleanse and correct the filth of my Conscience. Thou who comest from Heaven upon the Waters of thy Majesty, confirm this wonderful Sacrament in me.*

## TO OBTAIN THE GRACE OF THE HOLY SPIRIT

*Oh Lord my God, Father of all things, who revealest thy celestial and terrestrial secrets to thy Servants, I humbly beseech and implore thy Majesty, as thou art the King and Prince of all knowledge, hear my Prayers; and direct my works, and let my actions prevail in Heavenly virtues, by thy Holy Spirit: I cry unto thee, Oh God, hear my Clamor; I sigh to thee, hear the sighings of my Heart, and always preserve my Spirit, Soul and Body, under the Safeguard of thy Holy Spirit; Oh God thou Holy Spirit, perpetual and Heavenly charity, whereof the Heaven and Earth is full, breathe upon my operation; and what I require to thy honor and praise, grant unto me; let thy Holy Spirit come upon me, rule and reign in me, Amen.*

# TO RECOVER INTELLECTUAL WISDOME

*Oh Lord, I thy Servant confesse myself unto thee, before the Majesty of thy glory, in whose Spirit is all Magnificence and Sanctimony: I beseech thee according to thy unspeakable Name, extend thy merciful Ears and Eyes to the office of my operation; and opening thy hand, I may be filled with the grace I desire, and satiated with charity and goodness; whereby thou hast founded Heaven and Earth, who livest, &c.*

Say these Orations from the first day of the month, to the fourth day: in the fourth day Alpha and Omaega, and that following it, viz. Helischemat azatan; As it is in the beginning: afterwards say,

*Theos Megale patyr, ymas, heth, heldya, hebeath, heleotezygel, Sabatyel, Salus, Telli, Samel, Zadaziel, Zadan, Sadiz Leogio, Yemegas, Mengas, Omchon Myenoym, Ezel, Ezely, Yegrogamal, Sameldach, Somelta, Sanay, Geltonama, Hanns, Simon Salte, Patyr, Osyon, Hate, Haylos, Amen.*

*Oh Light of the World, immense God, &c.*

## HEREBY IS INCREASED SO MUCH ELOQUENCE THAT NOTHING IS ABOVE IT

*Thezay lemach ossanlomach azabath azach azare gessemon relaame azathabelial biliarsonor tintingote amussiton sebamay halbuchyre gemaybe redayl hermayl textos sepha pamphilos Cytrogoomon bapada lampdayochim yochyle tahencior yastamor Sadomegol gyeleiton zomagon Somasgei baltea achetom gegerametos halyphala semean utangelsemon barya therica getraman sechalmaia balnat hariynos haylos halos genegat gemnegal saneyalaix samartaix camael satabmal simalena gaycyah salmancha sabanon solmasay silimacrotox zegas me bacherietas zemethim theameabal gezorabal craton henna glungh hariagil parimegos zamariel leozomach rex maleosia mission zebmay aliaox gemois sazayl neomagil Xe Xe Sepha caphamal azeton gezain holhanhihala semeanay gehosynon caryacta gemyazan zeamphalachin zigelaman hathanatos, semach gerorabat syrnosyel, halaboem hebalor halebech ruos sabor ydelmasan salior sabor megiozgoz neyather pharamshe forantes saza mogh schampeton sadomthe nepotz minaba zanon suafnezenon inhancon maninas gereuran gethamayh passamoth theon beth sathamec hamolnera galsemariach nechomnan regnali phaga messyym demogempta teremegarz salmachaon alpibanon balon septzurz sapremo sapiazte baryon aria usyon sameszion sepha athmiti sobonan Armissiton tintingit telo ylon usyon, Amen.*

*Azay lemach azae gessemon thelamech azabhaihal sezyon traheo emagal gyeotheon samegon pamphilos sitragramon limpda jachim alna hasios genonagai samalayp camiel secal hanagogan heselemach getal sam sademon sebmassan traphon oriaglpax thonagas tyngen amissus coysodaman assonnap senaly sodan alup theonantriatos copha anaphial Azathon azaza hamel hyala saraman gelyor synon banadacha gennam sassetal maga halgozaman setraphangon zegelune Athanathay senach zere zabal somayel leosamach githacal halebriatos Jaboy del masan negbare phacarnech schon nebooz cherisemach gethazayhy amilya semem ames gemay passaynach tagaylagamal fragal mesi themegemach samalacha nabolem zopmon usyon felam semessi theon, Amen.*

## THE THIRD PART, THE SIGN LEMACH

*Lemach sabrice elchyan gezagan tomaspin hegety gemial exyophyam soratum salathahom bezapha saphatez Calmiehan samolich lena zotha phete him hapnies sengengeon lethis, Amen*

## FOR THE MEMORY

*Oh great invisible God, Theos patyr behominas Cadagamias imas by thy Holy Angels, who are Michael, the Medicine of God; Raphael, the Fortitude of God, Gabriel ardens holy per Amassan, Cherubin, Gelommeios, Sezaphim gedabanan, tochrosi gade anathon, zatraman zamanary gebrienam: Oh fulness, Holy Cherubins, by all thy Angels, and by all thy glorious Archangels, whose Names are consecrated by God, which ought not to be spoken by us, which are*

*these: dichal, dehel depymon exluse exmegon pharconai Nanagon hossyelozogon*
*gathena raman garbona vramani Mogon hamas; Which humane Sense cannot*
*apprehend: I beseech thee, Oh Lord illuminate my Conscience with the splender of*
*thy Light, and illustrate and confirm my understanding with the sweet odor of*
*thy Spirit, adorne my Soul, reform my heart, that hearing I may under×stand,*
*and retain what I hear in my Memory. Oh merciful God, appease my bowels,*
*strengthen my Memory, open my mouth mercifully; temperate my Tongue by thy*
*glorious and unspeakable Name: thou who art the Fountain of all goodness, have*
*patience with me, and give a good Memory unto me, &c.*

Say these Orations in the fourth ☾ , viz. *Hely Schemath*, Alpha and
Omega, *Theos megale*. Oh Light of the world *Azalemach*, great God I
beseech thee: these ought to be said in the 8, 10, 12, 20, 24, 28, 30, and in
all these Lunations rehearse them four times; in the morning once, the
third hour once, the ninth once, and once in the evening; and in the
other dayes rehearse none, but them of the first day, which are Alpha
and Omega, Helyschemat, Almighty, incomprehensible, I adore thee; I
confess myself guilty: O Theos hazamagiel: Oh merciful Lord God, raise
up the senses of my flesh: Oh God of all being, and of all Kingdoms, I
confess Oh Lord this day, that I am thy Servant. Rehearse these
Orations also in the other dayes four times, once in the morning, once
in the evening, once about the third hour, and once in the ninth; And
thou shalt acquire Memory, Eloquence and stability fully, *Amen.*

### THE CONCLUSION OF THE WHOLE WORK, AND OF THE
### SCIENCE OBTAINED

*Oh God, Maker of all things; who hast created all things out of nothing; who hast*
*wonderfully created the Heaven and Earth, and all things by degrees in order, in*
*the beginning, with thy Son, by whom all things are made, and into whom all*
*things shall at last return: Who art Alpha and Omega: I beseech thee though a*
*sinner & unworthy, that I may attain to my desired end in this Holy Art, speedily,*
*and not lose the same by my sins; but do good unto me, according to thy*
*unspeakable mercy: who doth not to us after our sins, nor reward us after our*
*inequities, Amen.*

Say this in the end devoutly:

*Oh wisdome of God the Father incomprehensible, Oh most mercyful Son, give unto me of thy ineffable mercy, great knowledge and wisdome, as thou didst wonderfully bestow all Science to King Solomon, not looking upon his sins or wickedness, but thy own mercies: wherefore I implore thy mercy, although I am a most vile and unworthy sinner, give such an end to my desires in this Art, whereby the hands of thy bounty may be enlarged towards me, and that I may the more devoutly walk by thy light in thy wayes, and be a good example to others; by which all that see me, and hear me, may restrain themselves from their vices, and praise thy holyness through all Worlds, Amen.*

Blessed be the Name of the Lord, &c. rehearse these two Orations always in the end, to confirm thy knowledge gained.

## THE BENEDICTION OF THE PLACE

*Bless Oh Lord this place, that there may be in it Holy Sanctity, chastity, meekness, victory, holiness, humility, goodness, plenty, obedience of the Law, to the Father, Son, and Holy Ghost; Hear Oh Lord, Holy Father, Almighty eternal God; And send thy Holy Angel Michael, who may protect, keep, preserve and visit me, dwelling in this Tabernacle, by him who liveth, &c.*

When you would operate, have respect to the Lunations: they are to be chosen in those moneths, when the ☉ rules in ♊ and , ♏ ♈ ♌ ♎ ♉. In these moneths you may begin.

In the Name of the Lord beginneth this most Holy Art, which the most high God Administered to Solomon by his Angel upon the Alter, that thereby suddenly in a short space of time, he was established in the knowledge of all Sciences; and know, that in these Orations are contained all Sciences, Lawful and unlawful:

First, if you pronounce the Orations of Memory, Eloquence, and understanding, and the stability thereof; they will be mightily increased, insomuch that you will hardly keep silence; for by a word all things were Created, and the virtue of that word all created beings stand, and every Sacrament, and that Word is God.

Therefore let the Operator be constant in his faith, and confidently believe, that he shall obtain such knowledge and wisdome, in the pronouncing these Orations, for with God nothing is impossi×ble: therefore let the Operator proceed in his work, with faith, hope, and a constant desire: firmly believing; because we can obtain nothing but by faith; Therefore have no doubt in this Operation, whereof there are three species, whereby the Art may be obtained.

The first species is Oration and reason of a Godly mind, not by attempting a voyce of deprecation, but by reading and repeating the same in the inward parts. The second species is fasting and praying, for the praying man God heareth. The third species is chastity; he that would Operate in this Art, let him be clean and chast by the space of nine dayes at least; And before you begin, it is necessary that you know the time of the ☾ it is proper to Operate in this Art: and when you begin so sacred an Art, have a care to abstain from all mortal sins, at least while you are proceeding in this work until it be finished and compleated: and when you begin to operate, say this verse kneeling:

*Lift up the light of thy Countenance upon me, Oh Lord my God, and forsake not me thy Servant N. that trusts in thee*

Then say three times *Pater Noster*, &c. And assert that thou wilt never commit wilfull perjury, but alwayes persevere in faith and hope.

This being done, with bended knees in the place wherein thou wilt operate, say:

*Our help is in the Name of the Lord, who hath made Heaven and Earth: and I will enter into the Invocation of the most high, unto him who enlighteneth and purifieth my Soul and Conscience, which dwelleth under the help of the most high, and continueth under the protection of the God of Heaven: O Lord open and unfold the doubts of my Heart, and change me into a new man by thy love: be thou Oh Lord unto me true faith, the hope of my life, and perfect charity, to declare thy wonders.*

Let us pray: then say the Oration following:

*Oh God my God, who from the beginning hast Created all things out of nothing, and reformest all things by thy Spirit; restore my Conscience, and heal my understanding, that I may glorify thee in all my thoughts, words and deeds; through him who liveth and reigneth with thee forever, Amen.*

Now in the Name of Christ, on the first day of the Month, in which thou wouldst acquire Memory, Eloquence and Understanding, and stability thereof, with a perfect, good and contrite Heart, and sorrow for thy sins committed; thou maist begin to pronounce these Orations following, which appertain to the obtaining of Memory and all Sciences, and which were composed and delivered by the Angel to Solomon, from the hand of God.

The first and last Oration of this Art is Alpha and Omega: Oh God omnipotent, &c.

his following is an Oration of four Languages, which is this:

*Hely, Schemat, Azatan, honiel sichut, tam, imel, Iatatandema, Jetromiam, Theos: Oh Holy and strong God, Hamacha, mal, Gottneman, Alazaman, zay, zojeracim, Lam hay, Masaraman, grensi zamach, heliamat, seman, selmar, yetrosaman muchaer, vesar, hasarian Azaniz, Azamet, Amathemach, hersomini. And thou most Holy and just God, incomprehensible in all thy works, which are Holy just and good; Magol, Achelmetor, samelsace, yana, Eman,* and cogige, maimegas, zemmael, Azanietan, illebatha sacraman, reonas, grome, zebaman, zeyhoman, zeonoma, melas, heman, hathoterma, yatarmam, semen, semetary, Amen.

This Oration ought to follow the first of the ten above written.

## TO PERFORM ANY WORK

This is to follow the third Oration above:

*I confess, O Theos hazamagielgezuzan, sazaman, Sathaman, getormantas, salathiel, nesomel, megal, vnieghama, yazamir, zeyhaman, hamarnal amna, nisza, deleth, hazamaloth, moy pamazathoran, hanasuelnea, sacromomem, gegonoman, zaramacham Cades bachet girtassoman, gyseton palaphatos halathel Osachynan machay, Amen.*

This is a true and approved experiment, to understand all Arts and secrets of the World, to find out and dig up minerals and treasure; This was revealed by the Heavenly Angel in this Notory Art. For this Art doth also declare things to come, and rendereth the sense capable of all Arts in a short time, by the Divine use thereof.

We are to speak also of the time and place. First therefore, all these precepts are to be observed and kept; and the Operator ought to be clean, chaste, to repent of his sins, and earnestly desire to cease from sinning as much as may be; and so let him proceed, and every work shall be investigated into him, by the Divine Ministery.

When thou wilt operate in the new Moon, kneeling say this verse:

*Lift up the light of thy Countenance upon us, Oh God, and forsake us not, Oh Lord our God.*

Then say three times the Pater Noster: And afterwards let him vow unto God that he will never commit wilfull perjury, but alwayes persist in faith. This being done, at night say with bended knees before thy bed; Our help is in the Name of the Lord, &c. and this Psalm; Whoso dwelleth under the shadow of the wings of the most high, to the end; and the Lords Prayer, and the Prayer following.

*Theos Pater vehamans; God of Angels, I Pray and invocate thee by thy most Holy Angels Eliphamasay, Gelomiros, Gedo bonay, Saranana, Elomnia, and by all the Holy Names, by us not to be pronounced, which are these: do. el. x p n k h t li g y y. not to be spoken, or comprehended by humane sense; I beseech thee, cleanse my Conscience with the Splendor of thy Name; illustrate and confirm my understanding with the sweet savour of thy Holy Spirit: Oh Lord Adorne my Soul, that I may understand and perfectly remember what I hear; reform my Heart, and restore my Heart, and restore my sense Oh Lord God, and heal my bowels: open my mouth most merciful God, and frame and temper my Tongue to the praise and glory of thy Name, by thy glorious and unspeakable Name. O Lord, who art the Fountain of all goodness, and original of all piety, have patience with me, and give unto me a true understanding, to know whatsoever is fitting for me, and retain the same in Memory: thou who dost not presently Judge a sinner, but mercifully expectest repentance; I beseech thee, though unworthy, to wash away the filth of my sins and wickedness, and grant me my petitions, to the praise and glory of thy Holy Name; who liveth and reignest one God in perfect Trinity, World without end, Amen.*

Fast the day following with bread and water, and give Almes; if it be the Lords day, then give double Almes; be clean in body and mind; both thy self, and put on clean Cloaths.

## THE PROCESSE FOLLOWS

When thou wilt Operate concerning any difficult Probleme or Question, with bended knees, before thy bed, make Confession unto God the Father; and having made the Confession, say this Oration.

*Send Oh Lord thy wisdome to assist me, that it may be with me, and labour with me, and that I may alwayes know what is acceptable before thee; And that unto me N. may be manifested the truth of this question or Art.*

This being done, Thrice in the day following, when thou risest, give thanks to God Almighty, saying;

*Glory and honour, and benediction be unto him that sitteth on the Throne, and that liveth for ever and ever, Amen.*

with bended knees and stretched out hands.

But if thou desirest to understand any book, ask of some that hath knowledge therein, what that book treateth of: This being done, open the book, and read in it, and operate as at first three times, and always when thou goest to sleep, write Alpha and Omega, and afterwards sleep on thy right side, putting the palme of thy hand under thy Ear, and thou shalt see in a dream all things thou desirest; And thou shalt hear the voice of one informing and instructing thee in that book, or in any other faculty wherein thou wilt operate: And in the morning, open the book, and read therein; and thou shalt presently understand the same, as if thou hadst studied in it a long time: And always remember to give thanks to God, as aforesaid.

Afterwards on the first day say this Oration:

*Oh Father, Maker of all Creatures; by the unspeakable power wherewith thou hast made all things, stir up the same power, and come and save me, and protect me from all adversity of Soul and Body, Amen.*

Of the Son, say:

*O Christ, Son of the living God, who art the Splendor and Figure of light, with whom there is no alteration nor shadow of change; Thou Word of God most high, thou wisdome of the Father; open unto me, thy unworthy servant N., the veins of thy saving Spirit, that I may wisely understand retain in Memory, and declare all thy wonders: Oh wisdome, who proceedest out of the mouth of the most high, powerfully reaching from end to end, sweetly disposing of all things in the World, come and teach me the way of prudence and wisdome. Oh Lord which didst give thy Holy Spirit to thy Disciples, to teach and illuminate their Hearts, grant unto me, thy unworthy servant N. the same Spirit, and that I may alwayes rejoyce in his consolation.*

## OTHER PRECEPTS

Having finished these Orations, and given Almes, when thou entrest into thy Chamber, devoutly kneel down before thy bed, saying this Psalm:

*Have mercy upon me, O God, according to the multitude of thy great mercies, &c. and, In thee Oh Lord have I trusted, &c.*

Then rise up, and go to the wall, and stretch forth thy hands, having two nayles fixed, upon which thou maist stay up thy hands, and say this Prayer following with great devotion:

*O God, who for us miserable sinners didst undergo the painful death upon the Crosse; to whom also Abraham offer'd up his Son Isaac; I thy unworthy servant, a sinner perplexed with many evils, do this day offer up and Sacrifice unto thee my Soul and Body, that thou maist infuse into me thy Divine wisdome, and inspire me with the Spirit of Prophesy, wherewith thou didst inspire the Holy Prophets.*

Afterwards say this Psalm;

*Oh Lord incline thine Ears unto my words, &c. and add, The Lord is my Shepherd, and nothing shall I want: he shall set me down in green pastures, his servant N., he shall lead me upon the waters of refreshment, he coverteth my Soul, and leadeth me N., upon the paths of his righteousness for his Holy Name: Let my evening Prayer ascend up into thee Oh Lord, and let thy mercy descend upon me, thy unworthy servant N., protect, save, blesse, and sanctify me, that I may have a shield against all the wicked darts of my enemies: defend me Oh Lord by the price of the blood of the just One, wherewith thou hast redeemed me; who livest and reignest God, whose wisdom hath laid the foundation of Heaven & formed the Earth, & placed the Sea in her bounds: and by the going forth of thy Word hast made all Creatures, and hath formed man out of the dust of the Earth, according to his own image and likeness; who gave to Solomon, the Son of King David inestimable wisdome; hath given to the Prophets the Spirit of Prophesy, and infused into Philosophers wonderful Philosophical knowledge, confirmed the Apostles with fortitude, comforted and strengthened the Martyrs, who exalted his elect from aeternity, and provideth for them; Multiply Oh Lord God, thy mercy upon me, thy unworthy servant N., by giving me a teachable wit, and an understanding adorned with virtue and knowledge, a firm and sound Memory, that I may accomplish and retain whatsoever I endevour, through the greatness of thy wonderful Name; lift up, Oh Lord my God, the light of thy countenance upon me, that hope in thee: Come and teach me, Oh Lord God, of virtues, and shew me thy face, and I shall be safe.*

Then add this Psalm: *Unto thee Oh Lord do I lift up my Soul: Oh my God in thee do I trust;* excepting that verse, *Canfundantur, &c.*

Having fulfilled these things upon the wall, descend unto thy bed, writing in thy right hand Alpha and Omega: then go to bed, and sleep on thy right side, holding thy hand under thy right Ear, and thou shalt see the greatness of God as thou hast desired.

And in the morning, on thy knees, before thy bed, give thanks unto God for those things he hath revealed unto thee,

*I give thanks unto thee, Oh great and wonderful God, who hast given Salvation and knowledge of Arts unto me, thy unworthy servant N., and confirm this Oh God, which thou hast wrought in me, in preserving me. I give thanks unto thee, O powerful Lord God, who createdst me, miserable sinner out of nothing, when I was not, and when I was utterly lost; and not redeemed, but by the precious blood of thy Son our Lord Jesus Christ; and when I was ignorant thou hast given unto me learning and knowledge: grant unto me thy unworthy servant N., O Lord Jesus Christ, that through this knowledge, I may be always constant in thy Holy service, Amen.*

These Operations being devoutly compleated, give thanks daily with these last Orations. But when thou wouldst read, study, or dispute, say,

*Remember thy word unto thy servant, O Lord, in which thou hast given me hope; this is my comforter in humility. Then add these Orations: Remember me O Lord of Lords, put good words and speech into my mouth, that I may be heard efficaciously and powerfully, to the praise, glory, and honor of thy glorious Name, which is Alpha and Omega, blessed forever, World without end, Amen.*

### THEN SILENTLY SAY THESE ORATIONS

*O Lord God, that daily workest new signs and unchangable wonders, fill me with the Spirit of wisdome, understanding and Eloquence; Make my mouth as a sharp Sword, and my Tongue as an arrow elected, & confirm the words of my mouth to all wisdome: mollify the Hearts of the hearers to understand what they desire, Elysenach, Tzacham, &c.*

# THE MANNER OF CONSECRATING THE FIGURE OF MEMORY

It ought to be consecrated with great faith hope and charity; and being consecrated, to be kept and used in Operation as followeth.

On the first day of the new Moon, having beheld the new Moon, put the Figure under your right Ear, and so consequently every other night, and seven times a day; the first hour of the morning say this Psalm, *Qui habitat, &c.* throughout; and the *Lords Prayer* once, and this Oration *Theos Patyr* once in the first hour of the day: then say this Psalm, *Confitebor tibi Domine, &c.* and the *Lords Prayer* twice, and the Oration *Theos Patyr* twice.

In the third hour of the day say this Psalm *Benedicicat anima mea Dominum, &c.* the Lords Prayer thrice, and the Oration Theos Patyr.

In the sixth hour say this Psalm: *Appropinquet deprecato mea in conspectu tuo Domine, secundun eloquium tuum.*
*Grant unto me Memory, and hear my voyce according to thy great mercy, and according unto thy word grant Eloquence, and my lips shall shew forth thy majesty, when thou shalt teach me thy Glory: Gloria patria, &c.*
Say the *Lords Prayer* nine times, and *Theos Patyr.*

In the nineth hour say the *Psalm Beati immaculati in via;* the *Lords Prayer* 12 times, and *Theos Patyr.*

In the Evening say this Psalm, *Deus misereatur nostri:* the *Lords Prayer* 15 times, and *Theos Patyr* as often.

The last hour say this Psalm, *Deus Deus meus respice in me, &c.*, and *Deus in adjutorium meum intende,* and *te Deum Lauadamus;* the *Lords Prayer* once, and *Theos Patyr:* then say the Oration following twice.

*O God, who hast divided all things in number, weight, and measure, in hours, nights and dayes; who countest the number of the Stars, give unto me constancy and virtue, that in the true knowledge of this Art N., I may love thee, who knows the gifts of thy goodness, who livest and reignest, &c.*

Four days the Figure of Memory ought to be consecrated with these Orations.

## O FATHER OF ALL CREATURES, OF THE SUN AND THE MOON

Then on the last day let him bath himself, and put on clean garments, and clean Ornaments, and in a clean place, suffumigate himself with Frankincense, and come in a convenient hour in the night with a light kindled, but so that no man may see thee; and before the bed upon your knees, say this Oration with great devotion.

*O most great and most Holy Father,* seven or nine times: then put the Figure with great reverence about your Head; and sleep in the bed with clean linen vestments, and doubt not but you shall obtain whatsoever you desire: for this hath been proved by many, to obtain such coelestial secrets of the Heavenly Kingdom are granted, Amen.

## THE ORATION FOLLOWING OUGHT TO BE SAID AS YOU STAND UP

*O great God, Holy Father, most Holy Sanctifier of all Saints, three and one, most high King of Kings, most powerful God Almighty, most glorious and most wise Dispensor, Moderator, and Governour of all Creatures, visible and invisible: O mighty God, whose terrible and most mighty Majesty is to be feared, whose omnipotency the Heaven, the Earth, the Sea, Hell, and all things that are therein, do admire, reverence, tremble at, and obey.*

*O most powerful, most mighty, and most invincible Lord God of Sabaoth: O God incomprehensible; the wonderful Maker of all things, the Teacher of all learning, Arts and Sciences; who mercifully Instructest the humble and meek: O God of all wisdome and knowledge, in whom are all Treasures of wisdome, Arts and Sciences; who art able instantly to infuse Wisdome, Knowledge and Learning into any Man; whose Eye beholdeth all things past, present, and to come; who art the daily Searcher of all hearts; through whom we are, we live and dye; who sittest upon the Cherubins; who alone seest and rulest the bottomless pit: whose Word gives Law throughout the universal World: I confess myself this day before thy Holy and glorious Majesty, and before the company of all Heavenly virtues and Potentates, praying thy glorious Majesty, invocating thy great Name, which is a Name wonderful, and above every Name, blessing thee O Lord my God: I also beseech thee, most high, most omnipotent Lord, who alone art to be adored; O thou great and dreadful God Adonay, wonderful Dispensator of all beatitudes, of all Dignities, and goodness; Giver of all things, to whomsoever thou wilt, mercifully, aboundantly and permanently: send down upon me this day the gift of the grace of thy Holy Spirit. And now O most merciful God, who hast created Adam the first man, according to thy image and likeness; fortify the Temple of my body, and let thy Holy Spirit descend and dwell in my Heart, that I may shine forth the wonderful beams of thy Glory: as thou hast been pleased wonderfully to operate in thy faithful Saints; So O God, most wonderful King, and eternal glory, send forth from the seat of thy glorious Majesty a seven-fold blessing of thy grace, the Spirit of Wisdome and Understanding, the Spirit of fortitude and Counsel, the Spirit of knowledge and Godliness, the Spirit of fear and love of thee, to understand thy wonderful Holy and occult mysteries, which thou art pleased to reveal, and which are fitting for thine to know, that I may comprehend the depth, goodness, and inestimable sweetness of thy most immense Mercy, Piety and Divinity. And now O most merciful Lord, who didst breathe into the first Man the breath of life, be pleased this day to infuse into my Heart a true perfect perceiving, powerful and right understanding in all things; a quick, lasting, and indeficient Memory, and efficacious Eloquence; the sweet, quick and piercing grace of thy Holy Spirit, and of the multitude of thy blessings, which which thou bountifully bestowest: grant that I may despise all other things, and glorify thee alone, the God of all things, the only true and perfect good, that I may forever glorify, praise, adore, bless, and magnify thee the King of Kings, and Lord of Lords; and always set forth thy praise, mercy and omnipotency: that thy praise may alwayes be* in my mouth, and my Soul may be inflamed with thy Glory for ever before thee. O thou, who art God omnipotents, King of all things, the greatest peace and perfectest wisdome, ineffable and inestimable sweetness and delight, the unexpressable joy of all good, the desire of all the blessed, their life, comfort, and glorious end; who was from eternity, and is and ever shall be virtue invincible, without parts or passions; Splendor and glory unquenchable; benediction, honor, praise, and venerable glory before all Worlds, since and everlastingly time without end, Amen.

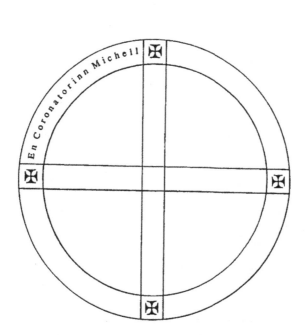

## THE FOLLOWING ORATION HATH POWER TO EXPELL ALL LUSTS

*O Lord, Holy Father, omnipotent aeternal God, of inestimable mercy and immense goodness; O merciful Jesus Christ, repairer and restorer of mankind; O Holy Ghost, comforter and love of the faithful: who holdest all the Earth in thy fingers, and weighest all the Mountains and Hills in the World; who dost wonders past searching out, whose power there is nothing can resist, whose wayes are past finding out: defend my Soul, and deliver my Heart from the wicked cogitations of this World; extinguish and repress in me by thy power all the sparks of lust and fornication, that I may more intentively love thy works, and that the virtue of the Holy Spirit may be increased in me, among the saving gifts of thy faithful, to the comfort and salvation of my Heart, Soul, and Body. O most great and most Holy God, Maker, Redeemer, and Restorer of Mankind; I am thy servant, the Son of thy hand-maid, and the work of thy hands: O most merciful God and Redeemer, I cry and sigh before the sight of thy great Majesty, beseeching thee, with my whole Heart, to restore me, a miserable sinner, and receive me to thy great mercy; give me Eloquence, Learning, and Knowledge, that those that shall hear my words, they may be mellifluous in their Hearts; that seeing and hearing thy wisdome, the proud may be made humble, and hear and understand my words with great humility, and consider the greatness and goodness of thy blessings, who livest and reignest now and forever, Amen.*

Note, that if you desire to know anything that you are ignorant of, especially of any Science, read this Oration: *I confess myself to thee this day, O God the Father of Heaven and Earth*, three times; and in the end express for what you desire to be heard; afterwards, in the Evening when you go to bed, say the Oration *Theos* throughout, and the Psalm *Qui Habitat*, with this versicle, *Emitte Spiritum*; and go to sleep, and take the Figure for this purpose, and put it under the right Ear: and about the second or third hour of the night, thou shalt see thy desires, and know without doubt that which thou desirest to find out: and write in thy right hand Alpha and Omega, with the sign of the Cross, and put that hand under thy right Ear, and fast the day before; only once eating such meat as is used on fasting dayes.

*SO ENDETH THE FIFTH BOOK CALLED*

*ARS NOTORIA.*

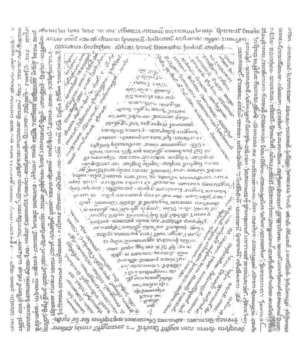

1st Notae,
Art of Grammar

2nd Notae,
Art of Grammar

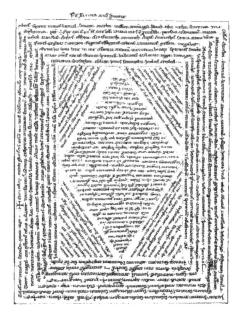

THE LESSER KEY OF SOLOMON

# LEMEGETON

BOOKS I, II, III, IV, V

*INDEX*

ARS THEURGIA GOETIA - BOOK II

SO ENDETH THE LEMEGETON.

Made in the USA
Las Vegas, NV
03 January 2025

15812974R00187